The Half Made Whole

THE HALF MADE WHOLE

JULIE WISEMAN

Copyright© 2018 Julie Wiseman

First published 2018

This book is copyright. Apart from any fair dealing for the purpose of private study, research, criticism or review, as permitted under the Copyright Act, no part may be reproduced by any process without written permission. Inquiries should be made to the author.

Typeset by BookPOD
Cover image by iStockphoto

ISBN: 978-0-646-99096-5
eISBN: 978-1-922270-05-4

To my beloved family.
To Robert, whose belief in this book gave me
the ongoing encouragement to write it.
And to our three precious children, Peter, Katrina
and Stephen who have contributed in their own
unique ways to my happiness and wholeness

Finally to my twin sister who has been my constant
companion and friend from before we were born.

Contents

Preface ix

Peas in a Pod
Born a twin 3
Struggle for personal identity 9

"Tu Palla Wan Taipim"
Emergence of individuality in Papua New Guinea ... 21

Red Heart
Adventures in Alice Springs 39
The reality of curses 53

Search for Spiritual Identity
Awakenings 63
Christian roots 65
Samplings of the East 70

Waking up in India
Waking up in India 77
Slippery slope 92
Seek and you will find 95
Hope in a horse trough 103
Nocturnal visitor returns 106
Ray of light 111
Beyond the veil 117

Healing the family tree

Healing the family tree 127
Time to sift and sort 151
A little visitor 154
More seeking 161
Surprising discovery 168
Root loosening 180
Plunging into the Tiber 183
Terrorism in America 187

Mid-life in the Middle Kingdom

The black dog bites 199
The first thread 207
Bamboo forest 218
Dentist in China 222

Pain in the Neck

A heartbeat away 227
The lump 229
The operation 233
The disease takes hold 239
Rapid recovery 247

Finding My Vocation

The half person no longer 253

Preface

My struggle for a personal identity began before I was born, within the womb of my mother. There I had to compete with my twin sister to receive enough of the nutrients to survive. The psychological and spiritual struggle to become a whole person was to take a lot longer.

It has been a meandering journey that led me all over the world and included some strange and unusual experiences. Through it all I grew in awareness that everyone struggles to a greater or lesser degree with these same issues.

So five years ago, when time finally allowed, I began to write about this journey.

I shared some of the experiences with an international writers' group while living in China, just so that I could contribute something to the group. To my surprise and delight, the members of the group liked what I had written and wanted to know more. With their encouragement and the constant urging from my husband, I dared to dream about a book. Like being on the journey, it has been fascinating to draw together all that has happened to have my longings fulfilled.

My hope is that this story may inspire others to find some answers too.

Peas in a Pod

Born a twin

For two short days at the very beginning of life my sister and I were a single cell. Then, somewhere between the fallopian tubes and the womb of my mother, something unexplainable occurred. Our one cell, known as a zygote, split in half. No one can explain why this happens. It remains a mystery. Technically it is a malfunction of the normal development process. So in between a mystery and a malfunction, my sister and I were formed.

Identical twins can share a placenta or each develops their own, depending on when the egg splits. If it is early enough, the two embryos will implant separately in the uterus and develop individual placentas. But if the split occurs later, they will share the placenta – as was the case with me and my sister. From that moment we were in competition to obtain enough nourishment from this one placenta to survive and flourish. My sister beat me at it as she was two pounds heavier than me at birth.

She also beat me into the world by 20 minutes. Not a very big time gap at all, but enough to have a dramatic impact on our lives. Anne used the 20-minute lead when we were kids to try and boss me around because she was the oldest! A more significant consequence involved my mother.

Mother had a very close attachment to *her* mother, Elsie,

who had a close bond with her sisters, Ellen, Ethel and Edie. Elsie, my nana, was born in the late 19th century, and like many women of that era was very talented in the ladylike pursuits of sewing, embroidery, tapestry, tatting and crochet. As Mother was growing up, she loved to visit her aunts who lived together in a beautiful house near Elwood beach. Nana and her sisters would sit in the elegant lounge room, chatting to each other while they did their various handiworks. Presently they would enjoy afternoon tea served in fine bone china cups with delicious homemade cakes, placed on hand-embroidered doilies edged with crochet lace. These were elegant, peaceful afternoons shared by the sisters.

My mother longed to share afternoons similar to that with her own sisters, but to her lifelong regret she only had brothers. After she married and delivered a son, the longing for more females in her family grew. When she discovered she was having twins, she begged Heaven to allow one of them to be a girl. Finally the wait was over and the day of our birth arrived. Into the world came the long-awaited girl, my sister Anne. Mother always said it did not matter what I was because she had her girl. She loved us both of course, but my sister's arrival gave her an edge in my mother's affections, and in the world, it seemed.

Anne and I shared the same genetic makeup and so looked very much alike. As our mannerisms were so similar, most people did not see us as individuals but rather grouped us together as the "look-alike twins". Back in the early 1950s multiple births were quite uncommon. To help people to tell us apart, Mum tied different coloured bows in our hair, a blue one for Anne and a pink one for me. I was therefore known as the "pink girl" and my sister as the "blue girl". This was our individuality. Before we had enough hair for tying bows, little gold name brooches were pinned to our clothes. Even wearing these brooches, or perhaps it was during a time when they were left off, I was given two doses of medicine while Anne had none; or perhaps it was the other way around.

During our childhood, Nana made most of our clothes. Two of everything: two identical turquoise coats with white fur trim, matching bonnets and muffs. Cotton dresses, one pink, one blue, with bows at the back. Little fluffy hand-knitted boleros with red tartan skirts. Anne's bolero and other articles of her clothing had an extra tiny flower embroidered onto it so that we could distinguish them. It was just accepted that Anne had the extra flower. These seemingly insignificant details had an influence on the way we perceived ourselves.

"Hey, Twinny, ... Anne, Julie, whichever one you are ..."

We were usually known as the "twinnies" and we were always together. In school and out of school we were involved in the same activities. The leaders of each activity developed strategies to tell us apart. At Brownies and Guides we were put into different units. I was in the Pixies, Anne in the Elves. At calisthenics we were usually in the front row. Anne's spot was on the left, mine on the right, with a girl in the middle. The teacher could then call out the correct name – unless we were feeling naughty and decided to swap places. The rest of the girls thought this was a great trick. After grade three at school, Mother insisted that we be put into different classes. Occasionally, to liven things up, we would swap classrooms. Sometimes the teachers never knew, but more often than not the constant giggles of the other students gave it away and we usually ended up being returned to our correct classes.

Our eccentric piano teacher, who had wiry, grey-peppered hair that she constantly tried to tame with bobby pins, bore the self-descriptive name of Mrs Wild. To ensure that she knew which twin she was teaching, she made certain that we had different music pieces to learn. Anne would learn Sonata in C and I would learn Sonata in B.

The separate class strategy came to an end when we moved to a new school. At 12 years old we were put in the same class again. We were a lively pair when we were together. We had the ability to know exactly what the other was thinking and could explode into insuppressible giggles at just a glimpse at each other. Of course, we would try desperately to stop, but if you have ever tried to overcome a fit of the giggles you will understand how impossible it is. It was like thousands of effervescent bubbles being suppressed by a little metal top. If you slightly loosened the top, out exploded the bubbles. Our giggles could disrupt the whole class and we often found ourselves at the principal's office for a serious talking-to.

The headmistress was stern but kind enough to realise that we were not cheeky or rude but just high spirited. One time, however, we found ourselves in the headmistress's office and she was very cross with us.

"Your teacher has just brought me the papers from your last English exam," she explained in a strict tone of voice. "She is very disappointed with you girls."

Anne and I looked at each other to see if either of us knew what she was talking about, but we were perplexed.

"I'm sorry, Mrs Miller, but we don't know what you mean," said Anne on behalf of us both.

"See here," she said, laying out our exam papers on her large mahogany desk. "First of all, you got exactly the same mark, which I suppose is understandable. But what gave your cheating away was that you wrote the same story for the composition section."

We stood silently for a moment, thinking about what she had said. Then we answered together, which was normal for us. "But, Mrs Miller, we were sitting on the opposite sides of the room from each other. So how could we have copied?"

Mrs Miller slowly sat down in her chair behind the desk and looked at us for what seemed like a long time. We stood meekly in front of her, unable to offer any explanation. Maybe she was trying to work out how we could have done it. But there was no way we could have copied anybody's work, let alone that of someone on the other side of the room, as the exams were very closely supervised.

"Well, I can't figure it out at all," she finally acquiesced. "We might just have to put it down to one of those mysterious 'twin things'."

Studies on identical twins were only just beginning and so we were brought up in the accepted way at the time. The expected thing to do was to dress twins alike, so we dressed like clones of each other until we were 15 years old. The problem was that when we were able to decide on our own clothes style, I was stumped. I could not decide what I liked. Anne didn't have this dilemma and so I relied on her for my fashion choices. She never agreed with the clothes that I gravitated towards, so I opted to go with what she liked, assuming that my choices were wrong. She was more popular than me and continually attracted compliments from people, so she had to be right. It was not until I was 21 years old and had moved away from home that I discovered my own dress style. Interestingly, it turned out to be very different from Anne's style. Over the years this has continued to be an external statement of our individuality.

Struggle for personal identity

Even though we were genetically identical, there were differences. Anne was a little taller.

"Anne got the steak and you got the lettuce leaves before you were born," Mum used to say.

One day we measured our bodies and discovered that the only difference in our height was in the length of our thighs. Hers were half an inch longer and I always thought she looked better because of it. (As middle-aged women, we discovered that Anne always thought of herself as tall and I always thought of myself as short. I still wonder what could be the significance of this perception!)

The most commonly asked question of identical twins is: "What's it like to be a twin?"

We would answer quite honestly:

"What's it like not to be?"

For most of my life I had unconsciously been mimicking Anne as I believed she was what I should be like, because she was ... just better than me! She was more like a whole person whereas I felt like only half a person. Anne initially beat me in everything, even if just by one mark, and received the higher awards at our various activities – except for one very precious time when we were seven years old. A few days before our calisthenics class was to be judged for the end of year awards, Anne had an accident which prevented her from participating. While visiting our cousin's house, Anne was outside and I was inside playing with a train set. Suddenly I jumped up needing to find my sister immediately. I tore outside yelling Anne's name. My mother and aunt, caught up by the panic in my voice, followed me. There was poor Anne sobbing in great pain. She had fallen off a scooter and was lying on the footpath with a broken elbow tucked beneath her. It was a bad break that needed an operation and metal pins to fix. (Poor Mother watched me closely for months, knowing of our tendency to have the same sorts of injuries.) On the day our calisthenics class was being judged for the awards, it was the first time in my whole seven years of life that I was not competing with Anne. A week later at the awards night, I proudly walked along the stage, while everyone clapped, to receive a gold medal for winning first prize in the Baby Junior section.

People continually confused us, as we were identical. But for reasons I could never quite understand, only Anne received the compliments, especially about her looks. One example sticks in my mind, as it represents a number of similar episodes. We were about 15 years old and were standing around with a group of girls in the school quadrangle. I noticed one of the girls staring at Anne. In the middle of the conversation she blurted out, "Haven't you got the biggest, prettiest blue eyes?" The other girls turned to admire my sister and agreed that she did.

At this age to be admired by your peer group was tantamount to being elevated to stardom. I opened up my eyes as wide as I could, wishing I could use my fingers to pull them even wider. I begged, not so much with my voice, which had to appear uninterested, but with my heart and soul, "What about mine?"

The girl, who was still admiring Anne, glanced at me dismissively.

"Yours are blue, but Anne's are so big and even bluer."

At that all the girls nodded enthusiastically. I nodded too with a smile so forced that the muscles in my cheeks reacted with a tremor. It reverberated down into my heart. I pleadingly glanced around the group to check if anybody noticed me. While their eyes were still glued to Anne, I backed out of the group, still nodding, the smile dissipating. I ran to the cubicle at the far end of the toilet block, closed the door behind me and I slunk to the floor feeling weak and dejected. I took deep gulps of air to steady all the emotions that were combating my self-control. I had not had enough time to recuperate. The last time something like this happened had only been less than a week before, at house sports.

House athletic sports were taken very seriously in our school because the athletes for the combined school sports were chosen based on these performances. Combined school sports were held at Olympic Park a few weeks later. Anne and I were natural athletes. We loved running, jumping, ball games and swimming. Today I think back and marvel at all the energy and skill that exuded from our young bodies. Anne could usually beat me by about one-tenth of a second on the track, about a metre. Interestingly, whenever we ran separately, my times were better than when we ran together. It was as if I prevented myself from beating her. An internal saboteur; I could not locate it nor stop it.

A year previously at the house sports I had pleased Miss

Davis, the physical education teacher, by winning the long jump and even breaking the school record. Anne had won the high jump but I had my long jump title and I didn't have to share with anyone. The glow remained with me all year.

One year on and I was determined to do it again. There were two girls chosen to represent our "blue team", Mandy and myself. At the last moment Mandy hurt her ankle and had to pull out of the competition. We needed someone to replace her and without any hesitation Miss Davis chose Anne. The previous day Anne had again won the high jump title for blue team. An hour later, Anne held my long jump title and had beaten my record. I sat through the applauding and presentation and then slunk into the dressing room. I knew I would have to endure it all again in the retelling at home and I needed some space to settle myself down. As we shared a bedroom, any tears I had were interpreted as jealously or oversensitivity. I thought the comments were probably right. I should have been happy for my sister. On one level I *was* happy because we were very close and I loved her deeply. But what my head was trying to tell me and how my heart reacted was similar to magnetic poles pushing violently against each other. I was desperately trying to feel as valuable in the world's eyes as Anne, but with each one of these incidents, this became harder to maintain.

Each year before the big inter-school sports, the fastest runner in the school was chosen for the 100 metre open sprint. For the last three years of secondary school, that meant it was between Anne and me. The first year this final race was held at lunchtime. Most of the school came out to see which twin was the fastest. We heard that bets were being made. The pressure was enormous. A number of false starts to delay our public competition only added to the tension. Then we schemed to finish at the same time. When this seemed too obvious, one of us feigned a fall. We were trying to delay the inevitable judgement. With our procrastination, the 12-second race lasted all lunchtime, until the teachers lost patience.

The following year, Miss Davis decided to hold the race after school so there would not be an audience. Surprisingly, many girls waited behind to witness the glory of one twin, who of course was Anne – another disappointment for me.

However, we knew how to have fun with looking alike. The girls at school used to fully enter into the spirit of the game when we would swap classes to fool the teachers. On a number of occasions I took detention in place of Anne because otherwise she would have had to forfeit playing in her sports team that afternoon. Everyone in our year level, except the teachers, knew of the conspiracy and for the most part joined in the deception.

A favourite lunchtime activity in the schoolyard was for various groups of girls to play the "let's spot the difference in the twins" game. They would stand us together side by side and then would begin to compare us. We knew all the things they would pick on so we were ready with our repetitive responses.

"They're exactly the same height," said one of the girls who thought she was making a profound statement.

"Actually, I'm taller," sighed Anne for the millionth time.

"She's 20 minutes older, so she got a head start," said I for the zillionth time.

"Oh really!" exclaimed the measuring group as one voice, believing that we'd just let them into one of the mysteries of twin growth.

"I think this one's skinnier," said another girl, while encircling my wrist with her thumb and index finger, before doing the same to Anne.

"Well, Mum says that I only got lettuce leaves and Anne got the steak when she was pregnant with us."

"Really?" chorused the group, becoming more fascinated.

We stood there side by side as the group dissected us further.

"Look, they've both got scabs on their knees in exactly the same places." We usually did have similar scratches, cuts and bruises in the same place. This we couldn't explain.

"I think this one's definitely got more freckles and her hair is a bit longer," was another usual point of distinction, even though the length of hair that day could be altered by the height at which we placed our pigtails. But these little details were never observed.

To finish off this familiar scenario, we liked to give them the grand finale. Anne would usually initiate it, signalling to me that she'd had enough of the "spot the difference" game.

"You see this scar on my elbow?" she would exclaim.

"Yeees," the girls would answer in unison.

"Well, this is where we were joined together before they separated us. Show them your scar, Julie."

I would dutifully show them a scar on the back of my knee that I had managed to acquire from a forgotten injury some years earlier.

"You are Siamese twins. Wow, that's amazing. If I hit you, then your sister would feel it. Right?" said the "know all" girl in the group. She slapped one of us on the arm, with the other one watching, who of course would then give the desired response of, "Ow."

Sometimes a group would be on to that, so they would make one of us turn around. But we could either hear the smack, or just know they were going to do it so we'd yell "ow" to acknowledge that the other had been hit. This always amazed them and would usually finish the comparison session. The group would leave us in peace as they walked away talking about the fascinations of Siamese twins. One day they would learn that Siamese twins are joined from the same place, usually from the torso or head. We hoped when they discovered this they would appreciate our joke.

When we started dating boys, we had a favourite trick. If a boy was arriving at our house for the first time to take Anne out, I would answer the door with a familiar greeting and a hug. He, believing it was Anne, would sometimes even plant a kiss. Then Anne would walk in. He, having been unaware that she was a twin, would be really flustered. After the explanation, everyone would laugh and the ice would be broken. It was also a way of checking out each other's partners.

During these years we went out with a set of identical twin boys, Greg and Sam. These boys were determined to marry twins, as they wanted to live close together all their lives and never be apart. Even though we were all only 16, I think they had decided that we were the twins for them. One Saturday afternoon the four of us headed into the city. We had decided to wear the same sorts of clothes for this planned expedition. Jeans, white skivvies, light blue V-neck jumpers and joggers. Greg and Anne walked down the street like any ordinary teenage couple and then Sam and I would hold hands and follow them a few metres behind. The reaction of the people along the street was exactly what we had wanted. Heads whipped around and then back to the other couple. People stopped walking and looked back and forth until they realised there really were two identical couples.

Sometimes we would do it on trams or trains. One couple would get on the vehicle. A few stops later the other couple would get on, making out we didn't know each other. We were good at keeping straight faces, as we watched the confused people around us.

We repeated this and other pranks a number of times over the months we went out with these boy twins, revelling in the attention it gave us. Looking alike was our identity. Apart, I didn't feel significant.

During our teen years the boys mostly wanted to go out with Anne, which was another reinforcement that she was just better than me, that she was the whole person who was more attractive, whereas I felt like only a half person. One time I went on a date with a boy who I thought was really cute. I was feeling quite flattered that he had asked me out, when over dessert he suddenly came out with, "I've actually only asked you out because I really wanted to go out with Anne, but she already has a boyfriend." Although this statement hit my heart like the many other heavy comparative stones that people threw at me, I couldn't find anything to say in my defence because I knew that it was true. Why settle for the half when you can have the whole?

The night of our 21st birthday party I made a decision. I had not intended to make it, but as the party progressed it became clear what I needed to do.

My parents had prepared a wonderful party for us in our home. Anne and I had been planning it for many weeks and were looking forward to our becoming officially adults. As the night progressed, Anne's girlfriends poured in, whereas mine trickled in. It was obvious to all that Anne was the popular twin. This was bad enough, but worse was still to come. I had invited one boy to the party, but everyone was noting the four charming young men hovering around my sister. This was humiliating enough already, but then halfway into the party the doorbell rang. Standing at the door was a surprise gift for Anne. He was a very handsome young man whom she had met on a holiday in Perth ten months earlier. She had flippantly mentioned her birthday coming up in ten months' time. She had obviously made such an impression on him that all these months later he had driven 3500 kilometres to be at her party. All her girlfriends were so impressed with this, which consequently elevated her to an even higher level in their esteem. So there was Anne with five charming young men vying for her attention and a roomful of admiring girlfriends. I felt so overshadowed and insignificant that I wanted to morph into the dark night forever.

As a twin I felt special and valued, but as an individual I felt insignificant, half a person. So as a statement of my age of maturity I decided that if I was to feel like a whole person, I needed to be in a place away from Anne and all those who knew me as a twin.

It would take me many years to find those elusive parts of myself that made me feel whole. I took the first big step on this journey when I accepted an invitation to spend three months in a remote village in Papua New Guinea.

"Tu Palla Wan Taipim"

Pidgin English for "twins": two fellows one type

Emergence of individuality in Papua New Guinea

my chance to spend some time away from my twin came while I was in college. During my second year of college I became very friendly with a young man, a fellow student. Konia had grown up in a small coastal village in Papua New Guinea about 290 kilometres east of Port Moresby. I had always been interested in other cultures, so I welcomed the opportunity to learn all I could about his way of life. He had dark brown skin and jet black frizzled hair in which he stored his pens and other small items. Another young man at the college was from a different part of PNG, the Island of Bougainville. He had almost black skin and a red tinge to his black hair.

Throughout the year I became immersed in Konia's culture as he gladly taught me some of his language and a variety of traditional dances and songs, as well as providing detailed explanations of his indigenous way of life. He had grown up in a coastal village where the men fished on outrigger canoes and the women tended gardens to grow their food. The village sounded like a big extended family that enjoyed a relaxed, unsophisticated way of life. He taught me some of his native dialect, as well as some pidgin English. This is a simplified form of speech that is usually a mixture of two or more languages. It has a rudimentary grammar and vocabulary and is used for communication between groups speaking different languages. It is also called *contact language*. Konia used to tease me by calling me the pidgin words for twin, *tu palla wan taipim*, which means two persons of one type. Quite descriptive really.

Konia was such an interesting and fun person to be with that I became infatuated with him and his tropical wonderland of a home. There was only one time I saw him without his broad contagious smile and that was when he told me about a deep sadness he carried. Konia had been sweethearts with a very beautiful girl since childhood. They had been engaged for a few months before he left to study in Australia. They were planning to marry on his return, following his graduation. Unfortunately she believed a jealous rumour that purported Konia was involved with someone else. Tragically she took her own life. He had postponed his studies for a year to grieve and now had returned to complete them.

As the year drew to a close Konia invited me to spend three months over the summer in his village among his family and friends. The idea of such an adventurous trip to a country that had become a youthful fantasy over the year was intoxicating. Boldly I accepted, joining him in the middle of December 1973. PNG had just begun self-rule a few weeks earlier. (A couple of years later they became independent of foreign rule.) Needless to say I had to overcome opposition from my parents who were very worried about my safety.

Konia assured them that the whole village would be my protection. I was dizzy with anticipation and unwilling to allow anyone to dissuade me from going, so to placate my parents I invited an older friend's husband to be my chaperone. He was an American scientist who jumped at the opportunity to examine the wildlife and flora in the area. So Kyle, with two cameras continually draped around his neck and a notebook in his hand, accompanied me. It was my first trip overseas and the biggest step I had ever taken without my sister.

The night I arrived in this tropical paradise, Konia and I walked to the top of a small mountain overlooking Port Moresby. As I gazed out over the ocean I experienced the most amazing sense of freedom and excitement. I was about to embark on a unique adventure into a village where no other white person had been. The adventurous part of me that had so far lain dormant stirred and awoke, destined to become a very definite part of my identity.

We stayed at one of Konia's sisters' house for a few days, which was in an outer suburb of Port Moresby. It was a very humble home that accommodated a number of their visiting relatives as well as myself and Kyle. The women all slept next to each other on the floor in one room, the men in another. A straw mat was the only thing between us and the hard floor. During the night I awoke to find a rat nibbling my finger but I was so exhausted from the unaccustomed humidity and the journey that I just pushed it away and went back to sleep. The next morning the men chased it out of the house by banging loudly on metal saucepan lids.

During the hot part of the afternoon the family gathered in the yard out back under the shade of a big tree where they had built a circular platform around a truck. It was an ideal place to gather lazily for talking and munching betel nut. I had noticed that a number of the people had red-stained teeth, which Konia told us was caused from chewing this nut.

"It's part of any social occasion, or we just chew it as part of our life here," he explained.

Kyle, the scientist, had done some research on it prior to the trip.

"It actually has a mild stimulant effect, but traditionally local people chew it for stress reduction, heightened awareness and to suppress hunger, which I suppose would be useful if food was scarce."

"I wondered what was in those hollowed out areca nut shells that most people wear over their shoulders. I assumed they were a type of small carry bag, not a place to store betel nut."

Konia went off with one of his brothers to buy some cold drinks as Kyle and I relaxed with the others. We watched as the adults dipped mustard sticks into a small container of lime, made from processed sea coral, and then into the areca shells that contained the betel nut. They drew the mustard sticks across the inside of their mouths, chewing the contents thoroughly while spitting the fibrous bits out of their mouths onto the ground, leaving little red patches. Everywhere we went there were these little red patches, spat indiscriminately around.

As I was sitting on the edge of the platform with my legs dangling over the edge, I felt another foot gently placed under mine. I looked up at the owner of these feet to see Konia's younger sister. She pointed to the rough logs underneath the platform, indicating that she was trying to protect my feet from hitting them. I experienced many such kindnesses from these gentle people.

Another day Konia and I went for a walk into a forested area some distance from where we were staying. After a while I wanted to sit and have a rest as the heat and humidity had again sapped my energy. Konia decided to leave me sitting on a log as he ventured a little further. He had been gone about ten minutes when out of nowhere came a man who then climbed up a nearby coconut tree. After coming back down he walked over to me, punctured the top of the young coconut in his hands, and gave it to me to drink. Then he just walked away. I had no idea who he was, but his unsolicited kindness warmed me even more to these people and this country.

A few days later we boarded an open utility truck to take us to Konia's village, called Allewai. Leaving Port Moresby we entered the thick tropical forest along a simple muddy road that had been forged by vehicles similar to our ute. It was a precarious journey lasting all day as a couple of times we came across roads so wet that we became bogged. At other times we drove off into the jungle to avoid oncoming traffic, which nearly bounced us out of the back of the open ute. Finally, right on dusk, we arrived at the village. Numerous corrugated iron huts elevated on stilts formed a large circle on the periphery of the forest. In the middle of this circle was an area of cleared land which was the gathering place for daily life and for festivals. All through the time I stayed in the village, this large dirt area was continually swept clean with brooms made of bundled up leaves tied together with plaited grass.

As the truck drove off into the elongated shadows of the jungle, the villagers wandered over to greet Konia and to see the *cinnabarra*, the white lady and the white man. The women had material wrapped around their waists called *ramies* which fell to their ankles. Their breasts were bare, which I thought was ideal in this hot sticky climate, and they wore beautiful necklaces made out of shells and seeds, which hung ornately on their rounded bosoms and nestled into their cleavage. Many had colourful hibiscus flowers stuck in their "fuzzy wuzzy" hair, making them even more exotic. The men also wore *ramies*, which only fell to their knees, while the children were naked. They giggled and hid behind their mothers when I smiled at them. Kyle and I would have seemed very strange to them with our Western clothes and light colouring. Over the coming days they would tentatively stroke my straight, light-coloured hair and hold their arms next to mine to compare the different shades of our skin. My blue eyes were a constant source of wonder and little brown faces would gather beneath me wanting to look into them.

I was puzzled by a particular thing they kept doing.

"Konia, I can understand the children finding my hair and eyes unusual, but why do they keep looking at my feet?"

"Ah. Well, as you can see, we don't wear shoes in the village and the children have never seen feet enclosed in sandals like you have on. They are wondering if white people have toes."

Looking down at my feet I wriggled my toes inside the sandals, and then gazing up at Konia, I returned his broad smile.

"Actually, Konia, I really need to use a toilet. Where is it?"

"I asked my brothers to make a private one for you just

near the hut. I thought you would find it more convenient. Come, I'll show you."

As I followed him to a hut with coconut trees behind it, I didn't think to ask him why it was more convenient. I was too intent on looking at this fascinating village in which I was going to live for the next few months.

Konia walked around to the back of the hut, and there in between a group of coconut trees was a small cubicle roughly built out of planks of wood. Inside was a stool. A circle had been cut in its seat. Underneath it they had dug a great deep hole.

We stayed in Konia's mother's hut. She did not know how old she was, but she'd had eight children and was grandmother to many more, so we calculated her to be in her late 70s. She wore a grass skirt and was rounded and wrinkled except for her breasts, which hung limply, flat after years of suckling babies. She could not speak any English and had never ventured far from her village. She offered us some young coconut juice, which was very refreshing in the hot climate, and some yams and freshly caught fish, which we ate with our fingers.

Konia divided the small hut into various rooms with rope and some spare *ramies*, which offered some privacy. Another sister was in one section with two small children snuggled up next to her. I could see her round belly protruding and realised there would soon be three little ones. Her husband was sleeping in another hut with his friends. We took up our positions by placing straw sleeping mats on the floor with our few possessions on top. During the day we rolled these up and took down the material to open up the hut. As the sun went down, the people went into their huts and soon all you could hear were jungle noises and the melodious crashing of the waves from the sea about 50 metres away.

The next morning at sunrise the village came to life. Without electricity village life followed the rhythm of the sun's rising and setting. Kyle and I headed down to the beach while people began their morning chores. I was quietly amused at my travelling companion and wondered how he and my friend had ever got together. She was an extrovert and full of energy and initiative while Kyle was reserved and rather vague. With his baggy long shorts, old-fashioned sun hat and glasses, he looked every bit an absent-minded professor. I could see his mind was occupied with assessing the environment as we walked along the beautiful beach lined with coconut palms that curved out over the sand.

While walking back towards the village we found a spot to sit for a while and gaze out to sea. Nearby were four narrow bridges extending out over the water for about 25 metres. They were made out of tree logs, with a little boxed room on the end. We watched as a number of people balanced their way out to the little rooms and after a while something would drop down out of the bottom of the room into the sea. Kyle and I were puzzled as we continued to observe this procession of people. After a while Konia joined us.

"Hi there. We've been watching a stream of people going out along those narrow little bridges and back again," said Kyle. "We can't work out what they're doing."

Konia started giggling before he answered.

"These are the village toilets!"

Aghast I swung around to stare at Konia, as Kyle fell backwards on the sand laughing uncontrollably.

It was only a few days until Christmas and preparations for a feast were beginning. Missionaries had brought Christianity to the area some time earlier, but it was neatly morphed with local ancestral worship. By the end of the day two enormous sea turtles lay on their backs on the shore. They had been caught for the Christmas feast but had to be kept alive for three days until it was time to kill and cook them. Without refrigeration food had to be collected and cooked immediately unless there was another way to keep it fresh. In the case of the sea turtles, they were kept alive by having buckets of water thrown on them periodically by a team of children. I felt so sorry for these poor creatures because as a city girl I was removed from the reality of how meat ended up on my dinner plate.

This ignorance became more manifest the next day. I was climbing down the small ladder out of the hut, when I saw one of Konia's older brothers and his mother sitting under the house plucking chickens. To my horror the creatures were alive and making the most pathetic sounds. Bursting into tears at the cruelty, I yelled, "What are you doing … they're still alive and they're in agony. Kill them now before you pull any more feathers out! Please, you have to kill them!"

Konia's mother and brother looked up at me unable to understand what I was saying but aware that I was upset. Hearing my raised voice, Konia arrived.

"You have to tell them to kill those poor birds. Can't they see how they're suffering?" I sobbed, appalled.

Konia relayed what I was saying and then they all burst into laughter.

Shocked at this reaction I turned and ran down to the beach. I could not understand how these gentle people could be so cruel. Standing ankle deep in the cool sea I was finally able to reflect calmly on the incident. In my society we had given feelings, intelligence and a soul to our animals. We became so attached to our pets that we almost thought of them as human. We were happy to eat meat as long as someone else killed it. But here I was in a so-called primitive culture where people's very survival depended upon them using everything possible for food. They could not afford to be emotionally attached to their animals. The pigs and their piglets that wandered freely around the village, which I thought were cute, were considered as future meals on legs. I felt embarrassed at my naive reaction in front of Konia's family, which I knew would cause some laughter among the villagers. I sniggered too at how they would picture me as a typical *cinnabarra* – which I obviously was.

The afternoon was very hot and we decided to go for a swim. Before coming to PNG I had swapped my bikinis for a one piece bathing suit, assuming that it would be more appropriate. I had been shocked, however, to see other white women walking around the streets of Port Moresby in their bikinis. I had assumed they would have been more sensitive to this different culture.

I stepped down out of the hut in my "modest" bathing suit feeling very superior to those other insensitive white women. But as I began to walk towards the beach, I noticed how everyone stared at me and some of the young women giggled behind their hands. I looked at Kyle who was also confused. Konia was not around to ask, so I did a quick assessment. The village women had all their legs covered down to their ankles while their breasts were uncovered. Here I was with all my legs uncovered and my breasts covered. I had it the wrong way around completely.

Embarrassed, I dived back into the hut and wrapped a *ramie* around my waist, emerging in more appropriate attire for the culture.

The following day it was market gardening day and I was joining the women in this task. Very early on in time, PNG women discovered how to clear spaces in the forest and to cultivate crops in the fertile soil enabling them to supplement their diet with fresh vegetables. During the last few nights I had been bitten by ferocious mosquitoes and the red welts showed up nicely on my white skin. One of the women came up to me and rubbed pig fat over my exposed skin, which stopped the mosquitoes from biting me. This was another of those thoughtful gestures that seemed to come naturally to these people.

As we walked into the forest towards the gardens, the women broke out into beautiful singing. The harmonies they naturally fell into were more complicated than the various parts of a song that my old school choir had learnt. It had taken us weeks of practice to get the harmonies right, and here were these village women sounding perfect without any musical notation to follow or choir conductor to keep the beat steady. When we arrived at the gardens, they taught me how to dig for the yams and other root crops which we carried back in multipurpose bags called *billums*, handwoven from plant reeds. To carry any item in *billums*, the women would put the handles around their foreheads with the bulk of the bag hanging on their backs. They would also hang them on low branches of trees and place their babies in them. The open weave kept the babies cool and the *billum* could be swung gently to soothe them.

On the way back from the gardens I had to sit down – it was so hot and I was drained from the heat. It was the wet season which brought the highest humidity of the year. A few of the women began to fan me with a palm frond. Then they taught me an important lesson about living in the tropics. They could not speak to me so they mimed the way I walked, which was briskly with arms swinging fast and furious. They all rolled on the sand laughing and then hugged me. Then one lady showed me how they walked, slowly with her torso relatively still and swaying from the hips. It looked very graceful so I stood up and copied her. Their clapping and cheering indicated that I had it. We all slowly swayed our way back to the village without the need to stop again.

On Christmas Eve the turtles were killed, along with a number of the pigs which I heard squealing at the end of the village. I did not go and watch. The women were preparing the food while the men organised the *mumu*. This is a slow cooking method where a large fire is built in a hole dug in the ground. When the fire dies to glowing red embers, the meat is wrapped in banana leaves and placed on the coals. Then it's covered back over with soil and left to cook overnight. I was constantly in awe at the ingenuity of these people who had devised ways of doing so many things to enhance their way of life without any of the modern implements that I took for granted. Here we had a slow cooking oven that could hold much more food than our electric oven at home, and the meat, I was to discover, was very tender and full of flavour.

At dawn on Christmas morning most of the villagers wandered along the white sandy beach to a neighbouring village where there was a church. I was now feeling like a real villager walking along arm in arm with a couple of the ladies. They were a very tactile people, not afraid to touch others of the same sex or to show affection. Some young men walked by hand in hand or with arms around each other. I felt so alive and unique in this environment. Not only did the people see me as an individual, but also as a unique and special person, as I was so different to the indigenous people. We walked along singing the songs that Konia had taught me. I yearned for this scenario and the accompanying feelings to last forever. Approaching the next village we could hear their beautiful island singing floating towards us. Arriving at the church the women went to the right side and the men to the left with an aisle between. We sat on the floor on grass mats while the breeze from the sea drifted through the open walls of the thatched roof building. The indigenous pastor preached and prayed. With my basic language skills, I did not understand much, but amused myself by watching the pastor's exaggerated gesticulating until everyone began to sing. Some of the songs I recognised as Christmas carols, but they were sung in that unique harmonising way that carries your emotions to exotic places.

Back in the village, the *mumu* was being opened and vegetables and fruits were laid out on big banana leaves. A couple of the young men had guitars and were singing while children danced around them. There was a bundle of smaller banana leaves in a pile which we used as plates, helping ourselves to the beautiful fresh food of yams, sweet potatoes and sago with green vegetables of bitter cucumber and *kumu*. The turtle meat tasted like a combination of chewy chicken and squid while the pork was very tender. A couple of the young lads climbed up the coconut trees so fast that I almost missed them. They used a little band of woven grass to keep their feet evenly apart and then pushed from their legs and pulled with their arms until they could reach the fruit. They threw the young coconuts down to be punctured at the top to pour out the refreshing milk. The fruits, which all grew near the village, had been cut and laid on some fresh banana leaves. We helped ourselves to pineapple, mango, guava and watermelon, followed by watermelon spitting competitions. The winner spat them the furthest.

After an hour of relaxing while the remains of the feast were cleared up, the sports began. There were children's foot races, coconut tree climbing races for the men and ball games. When it was time for the young women's race, I went up to where the competitors were gathering. I could see the looks on their faces as well as on those of the spectators. They assumed that the *cinnabarra* would not have a chance beside their women. I felt secretly confident as I acknowledged that in this race I was running as a single person instead of a twin. There was no psychological saboteur that in the past had prevented me from winning.

On the signal we ran up and around the furthest banana tree, through the village square and up past the final hut to the finish line. I figured it to be at least 150 metres. I felt I was flying as I ran barefoot around the circuit to the growing hoots and cheers of the spectators. I won the race by a significant lead and relished the loud applause of the surprised villagers. I felt elated and jumped up and down with excitement as the other girls hugged me and Konia picked me up and twirled me around. I think he may have been a bit proud of this *cinnabarra* he had brought home to his village. As I lapped up all the attention I perceived a shift occurring deep inside. I realised I felt less of the underbelly of a twin ship and more of an individual. For a brief moment I thought about Anne, enjoying her summer vacation from teachers college on an Australian beach. But no beach holiday, I thought to myself, could come anywhere near the experience I was having. These wonderful feelings of adventure and difference enveloped me and I fed on them greedily.

That evening the village square was decorated with flowers and people gravitated to where the dancing had begun. I had been given a grass skirt which exaggerated the movement of my hips as I began to dance the way Konia had taught me. It was very similar to a Hawaiian hula dance where you kept you knees and legs together, while swaying your hips by moving on the outside of your feet. I had found it difficult to master when Konia had originally taught me months earlier, but tonight all the practice had paid off and I danced like a true indigenous woman. Poor Kyle had absolutely no rhythm and so after a few attempts to simulate the way the men danced, to the hilarity of all, decided to opt for flashing away with his camera.

That night was full of magic for me. I danced with the women while the men, so full of rhythm and strength, danced their way around us. It was a tropical wonderland, untouched by white civilisation with the raw passion of young vibrant people losing themselves in the beat and harmonies of island singing and dancing. I felt so alive. I felt strong and competent.

I felt that the real me was emerging as I danced and sang and laughed until dawn.

Red Heart

Adventures in Alice Springs

In the centre of the Australian continent there is what is known as its "Red Heart". Not a physical beating heart, but rather a mystically beautiful desert with deep red earth, rich in sacred significance to the Aboriginal people who have lived there for over 50,000 years. These people knew the beat of this land and lived with its rhythms. After the white settlers arrived, a town grew up, known as Alice Springs, named after the wife of the South Australian Postmaster General at the time.

It was 1974 and I was employed as a youth worker in Melbourne. On Christmas morning, the most severe tropical cyclone in Australian history, Cyclone Tracy, flattened 80 per cent of the town of Darwin. As that was only 1500 kilometres north of Alice Springs, many of the survivors were evacuated there. The organisation I was working for asked if I could leave immediately to fly up and help with the refugees.

The building where I would be staying was about ten years old and built in the shape of a "U". On one side of the U was the hostel where a number of women boarded. On the other side was where the staff lived. When I was shown my accommodation I was very excited, since it was the first time in my life that I was going to have a room to myself instead of sharing one with my sister. It became my own private space, which allowed more of my individuality to begin to emerge. I decorated it the way I liked, turned the light off at night when I wanted and, most importantly, I had a place where I could laugh, cry or sulk in private without anyone knowing.

After settling in I went for a walk to familiarise myself with the area. Reaching the edge of town I paused. There it was before me, this huge inland desert as far as the horizon, without the interruption of a house or a fence or another person. I sat down under the shade of a white ghost gum tree as a screeching flock of pink-crested cockatoos flew above. When they had passed, it was silent again. An intense eerie silence was all around me. I listened to the silence and heard whispers in the wind, taking me back in time. I believed I could feel the country's heart pulsating from an ancient past, hiding its secrets, luring me to discover them. I leant back against the trunk of the tree, flicking a bull ant off my leg. The landscape was so dramatic in its contrast of brilliant blue sky against deep red earth, colours that were exaggerated by the inordinately bright sunlight.

An intense feeling of adventure and freedom permeated the innermost part of my being as the realisation of the situation hit me fully. Here I was on my own, over a thousand miles from home, answerable only to myself. People were going to know me as an individual rather than as one of the twins. No sooner had this realisation settled in my mind, than an image of Anne beginning her first year of teaching at a primary school in suburban Melbourne popped into my head and I wondered whether she felt the same as I did about us being apart from each other.

I stayed there for a long time thinking and taking it all in until I realised it was getting late. Dusk had fallen and the country turned a glowing red, as if on fire, so I left my ghost gum and hurried back into town and to my very own room.

Over the following weeks I met the other women who boarded in the U-shaped building of the YWCA. There was one group of five women who had come to Alice Springs from all over the country and with whom I became particularly friendly. Listening to the various stories and the reasons they chose to live and work in this remote part of the country, I was building a picture of "Alice" as a place where people came to escape from bad situations, or from themselves.

The town had very little traffic and the weather was warm and dry so the women chose to ride motorbikes. With a great deal of nagging from this group, I finally went and boldly purchased a Honda 90 step-through motorbike. It was lime green and I chose an orange helmet. Not exactly colour coordinated, but at least it ensured I would be seen. I had never ridden a motorbike before, so the salesman gave me a basic lesson on how to stop, start and change gears. Feeling confident, I rolled it out of the car yard, turned on the ignition, grabbed the throttle and with giddy excitement turned it to the full position. Immediately the bike stood up on its back wheel as I sped down the road, red dust and exhaust fumes exploding out behind. Frantically I released the throttle and the bike bounced down onto its front wheel at an angle and conked out, tipping on its side. Luckily it was a quiet country road; it took me quite a while to lift it back to an upright position. It was a relatively small bike, but

I was not a huge woman and it was just so heavy. Turning back towards the car yard, I saw my salesman still standing there, shielding his eyes from the glare of the sun, looking down the road towards me. As I waved to him to show I was alright, he shook his head, lit a cigarette and sauntered back into the yard.

I spent the afternoon practising all the manoeuvres needed to ride a motorbike and decided it was time to go for a spin with the "bikie group". They knew a great deal about the town, having lived there for a number of years. One member of the group, Marlene, was an Aboriginal. She was deaf in her right ear and had a slight speech impediment because of it. She told me that she had not been born deaf. It took a few drinks and a camp fire for her to open up about what had caused it.

I felt so uninhibited roaring along with my new friends. They had no idea that I was only half a person and they liked me and had included me in their exclusive group. In years gone by I had thought that without Anne I would not be able to manage. But here I was thousands of miles away from her and I was feeling strong and capable. A joyful sense of my adventurous and daring spirit had been fused into my personality and was a defining part of my individuality.

"That's the Todd River," Marlene yelled out over her shoulder as we rode along, sometimes three abreast, sometimes single file, depending on the road.

"What do you mean it's a river? It's as dry as a bone."

"Only has water in it when the rains come and that's only every few years or less."

We all pulled over one after the other until the five of us lined up along the riverbank. It was hard to imagine water running down this completely dry riverbed. All the way along I could see makeshift humpies and groups of Aboriginal people sitting around.

"Why are they setting up camp here, Marlene?"

"They leave their settlements in the bush to come 'ere. Some of 'em wants work, but gets into the grog. Some try to make it in the white man's ways, but it's so different to our ways it's like they give up. Mobs of 'em puts up shelters 'ere to drink and sleep it off."

I looked along the riverbed. It was dotted with these makeshift humpies under trees. They were made up of a few pieces of scrounged wood with branches on top for a roof. Some had bits of cloth to offer more shade. Some people lay sprawled out on the dirt, while others sat in groups, drinking out of bottles. I felt really sad and wanted to know how they could be left to live like this.

"So they're allowed to live here then?"

"Not really, but ya get rid of one mob and another mob moves in. Or they wait 'til the police 'ave done the raid and then come back. It's them drunk mothers that cause a problem. Ya can't look after ya baby when ya pissed outya brain, so the poor little buggars get left. Sometimes they freeze to death during the night or just get neglected and get real sick."

"Really ... that's ... that's just awful." The reality of life for the 20th century Aboriginal was not the romantic image I had learnt at school. These people had once been a proud race that was extremely adaptable and skilled, enabling them to live in this harsh, desert environment. They knew how to track the smallest animal, find water in the desert and to kill meat by throwing a piece of wood crafted in an ingenious way that ensured it would return to them if it missed their prey. What a clever way to save energy in this hot dry climate. They also had a profound spirituality which emphasised the necessity of living in harmony with and as part of the environment. But the people in the riverbed did not look proud but defeated and lost. Marlene continued with her appraisal of the situation.

"The police sometimes come down by surprise and end up taking them babies to get looked after. It makes them mothers real angry."

"Don't they get them back when they sober up?"

"Sometimes, but if they make a habit of it, the kids get fostered out indefinitely."

"I guess I can understand that."

"Yeah, but they're not white man's kids. People still remember when their kids was taken by force. They not done nothing wrong, but white missionaries and other government 'do-gooders' not like our ways cause we don't need big 'ouses and like living in the bush, like our ancestors. They don't want our kids to learn our ways, but send 'em to white man schools. Trying to turn 'em into white fellas."

As I observed the situation in the Todd, I think I understood what the government's intentions were, but through Marlene's eyes I learnt how difficult it had been for her people. I felt guilty being a white woman, especially when I realised that they had stopped taking the children away from their parents only four years before. These children were later known as "the stolen generation" and it took until 2008 for a politician to finally give the people a formal apology for having affected 85 per cent of Aboriginal families in this way.

Getting back on our bikes we decided to head out of town and have dinner around a camp fire. We grabbed some sausages, a billy, tea, flour, jam and water. After riding for about an hour we found a nice spot under three big ghost gum trees. Jo, a really masculine looking woman who rode the biggest bike of the group, dug a small hole and built the fire using fallen wood and bark from the trees. Susie helped her collect the wood and then poured water into the billy. She was a tallish young woman with wavy long honey-blonde hair and a shapely figure. She had been jilted by her fiancé a month before their wedding and to recover from her intense humiliation and broken heart chose remote Alice Springs. Maybe the barrenness of the surroundings reflected her feelings. But a week after she arrived she met Donna, herself finding solace in remote Alice Springs from a physically abusive marriage. Donna was of medium height and build, with greying hair shaved at the sides and short at the back. She always wore a large man's shirt over loose trousers, as if she were attempting to hide any outward sign of her femininity. Yet she was softly spoken and graceful, with green eyes that held within them the pain she sought to forget.

It had taken me some time to understand why Susie and Donna shared a room and never dated any men. There were plenty of single men in this part of Australia, as I had discovered through the many dates I had been on. (It was during my time in Alice that I made a conscious decision to see how many men I could date. This went on for a number of years and as my confidence grew so did the invitations. Sometimes I would have three young men interested in me at the same time, which really boosted my damaged ego. In retrospect, I realised that I was trying to prove to myself and others that I was as attractive to the opposite sex as was my sister. Years later, as healing came to this wounded part of me, I remembered this vow and was able to put an end to it.)

One evening I had gone to Susie and Donna's room to deliver some mail. It was the first time I had needed to go to their room as usually we met in the kitchen or in the garden. I saw their beds were pushed together and being quite naive back then I was puzzled. After a short conversation they explained to me that they had been together for four years and planned to spend the rest of their lives as a couple. They pointed to the matching wedding bands they wore on their fingers. As I walked back to my room another fact dawned on me. Jo was such a good friend and we had lots of fun together and yet whenever I was about to go on a date, she became very cold towards me and could be quite nasty. I had not been able to figure out why, but after my talk with Susie and Donna, I understood. Not long after that, Jo announced her love for me with a big embrace. I froze within her arms as I struggled to find a diplomatic answer, which she reluctantly accepted. Our friendship continued, but with more reserve.

Marlene was busy mixing damper in a small plastic bowl. By dusk the fire had died down to red-hot coals, around which we sat on the ground or stray tree branches. The surroundings glowed orange then crimson then purple as the sun set over the back of the MacDonnell Ranges. The gentle breeze had died off and all was still.

The billy started bubbling over, so I took a handful of tea leaves and plonked them into the water. After securely replacing the lid, I spun the billy around and around over my head and down to my knees like a windmill on its side until I reckoned it was brewed properly. We wrapped the damper dough around medium-sized sticks and held them over the coals, twisting the sticks constantly to ensure the inside was cooked as well. When it was ready, the damper slipped easily off the sticks and we poured jam into the holes. With a tin mug of hot billy tea, damper and sausages, we relaxed around the camp fire. In such a setting, it was hard to keep up external pretences. Soon the conversation began to deepen and we started sharing stories from our lives.

Marlene was unkindly called a half-caste. Her mother had been from the *Aranda* tribe that populated the areas around Alice Springs, and her father was a visiting geologist from England. Since her father had disappeared even before she was born, she was raised in her mother's community and had been educated by the nuns at a local mission school. She had dreamt of becoming a nurse. She was 24 and I thought she still had plenty of time, but she seemed confused and had an edge of despair.

"When I was a little four-year-old, my uncle came back from town real drunk. He was my favourite uncle. Used to give us mob lollies and play with us."

I had heard the Aboriginal people use this word "mob" to refer to anything greater in number than about five and now it had been incorporated into the local lingo.

"My uncle didn't drink, cause he reckoned it was destroying our people. But earlier that day he'd been told that old man Woorak from the other tribe had pointed the bone at him for takin' his son's woman."

I looked across at Marlene through the smoky haze of the camp fire. I was about to scoff with her about that superstitious practice, but she was looking into her mug of tea with no hint of amusement.

"But, Marlene, surely that pointing the bone stuff is all just primitive mumbo jumbo."

"No, it's real, very powerful," she whispered looking

deep into my eyes. "If the bone pointed at you, you will die."

"Oh come on now, if someone really believes that, then they would talk themselves into it working, right? It's psychological, mind over matter." I thought I was being smart and showing them that I was not going to let them play a joke on my gullibility.

I looked around the group, expecting to see one of them smirking, but they were all staring intently into the fire.

Donna looked up in my direction and with her gentle voice floating across the circle added, "There's more to it than that. When you've been here longer, you might understand a little more about the Aboriginal people. They have such a strong relationship to the land, for example. It's part of them. White men come and try to put them in houses, but they like living outside sleeping on their earth, looking at the sky. They draw their strength and life from their connection to the land. We think we know what's best for them, but we don't know them at all. We think we can explain their spirituality, but it is very sophisticated really and for the most part we don't get it."

Susie took up the explanation.

"Our cultures are so different. Whereas our culture concentrates on preparing ourselves for the future, like with our education system, preparing for a job, waiting to get married until you have enough money etc., their culture is about the past, the Dreamtime and its relevance to the present."

"Yes, OK, I accept that, but the curse stuff is a bit primitive. Isn't it just a people trying to explain why bad things happen in their world? I can't honestly believe that someone pointing a bone at another is really going to cause him to die!"

"The Kurdaitcha man uses a bone infused with special powers from a secret ceremony. No women are allowed to see this," Jo explained.

"The who?"

"The Kurdaitcha man. He's chosen by the elders to be the tribe's ritual executioner. He causes death and sickness as punishment to people who break blackfella law," explained Marlene.

"But was your uncle breaking the law, Marlene?"

"Well, yes. We 'ave very definite rules on who can marry who. Some tribes we can choose from, others we can't. Only people from this tribe can marry people from that tribe. But some tribes we not allowed to marry. In fact, if a girl is seen even lookin' at a boy from that tribe, she badly punished and same with a man if he even looks at woman from wrong tribe."

Jo started stirring the fire and then placed another small log on it as she continued this topic.

"Scientists have done studies on this. What they discovered was amazing. With the tribes that were not allowed to intermarry, it was found that genetically they were incompatible and it would have caused lots of birth defects or stillbirths. Now how did an ancient people know that things would not work out if they mixed these tribes?"

"I used to think like you," piped up Susie. "But I've seen things since living here that I cannot explain."

"So what happened to your uncle, Marlene?" I was beginning to feel outnumbered in my obvious ignorance. Then again maybe they had all lived here too long and were losing touch with reality. I could understand how it could happen. This outback land exuded an almost mystical atmosphere, with its isolation and extreme landscape.

"He died a week later, but not before he bashed me across the right side of me head and knocked me out. Didn't hear in that ear after that."

Stunned into silence at this we all looked into the fire and were comforted by its glow and the occasional crackling. Presently Donna almost whispered, "Why did he do that to you, Marlene? You were only a four-year-old child."

"I'd never seen 'im drunk, and I thought he was just playin' around. So I kept pestering 'im for lollies. I reckon he didn't know what he was doin' as he was so scared that the bone had been pointed at 'im, so he'd gone an' got drunk for the first time. When I kept pestering 'im, I guess he lost patience and whacked me."

"I suppose life could only get better after that," said Jo, trying to lift our spirits.

"Yeah, s'pose it did for a while. After I saw my uncle so drunk, I decided I wasn't gunna eva touch the bloody stuff. I also decided that I was gunna stay a virgin 'til I got married. No other woman I know had done this and I was determined to better meself and one day become a nurse. Stay a virgin and not drink. Pretty stupid thing to try an' do, right?"

"No, you go, gal," said Susie.

Jo went around the circle pouring more tea into our mugs from the billy. When she sat down, we became aware of a soft sobbing coming from Marlene. Suddenly she blurted out in between sobs, "Gees, it's a bugger. When I was 16, I went to a party with some friends on the back of a ute. On the way home they was all really plastered, 'cept me. The driver pulled up to take a leak and everyone jumped out of the ute and started running into the dark yelling and hooting. They was all just being idiots. I got out and found a bush for a pee. As I stood to pull up me undies, one of them drunk buggars jumped up from behind a bush and forced me to the ground and pushed his bloody big dick into me with such force that I screamed in pain. He shoved 'is hand over my mouth and raped me so hard I thought he was going to rip me insides up … When it was over he slumped onto me … I'll never forget the weight of 'is body or the stink of the booze as he panted into my face. His rotten sweat was all over me. I tried for days to wash it off, but it felt like it would never come off."

Her gut-wrenching sobs gradually eased. We all knew to leave her alone as she let it out. After a while all was silent except for the distant howl of a dingo.

"I lay there in the dark with 'im asleep on top of me, listening to the other idiots still laughin' and yelling. None of 'em knew that one of their own women had just had her dream shattered. I never cared who I was with after that."

I had tears in my eyes as I reached over to touch her hand, which was clenched on her knee, wet from the tears she had wiped off her face.

I could not think of anything to say that would not sound hollow. Gradually the others came over and we wrapped her in our hugs and womanly empathy.

"Well, at least I made it to 16. That's a lot older than most of the girls I know," she finally offered, I think mainly for our benefit rather than reflecting her true thoughts. "But I gave up on the idea of trying to become a nurse."

We all stayed silent in respect for the painful experience that had been shared.

Finally, through gritted teeth, we heard Marlene whisper

to the night and beyond, "Wished I'd got our elder to set the Kurdaitcha man on 'im."

After this night around the camp fire, I tried to rationalise the tales of the way evil spirits supposedly affected the living, stories like the Aboriginal practice of pointing the bone. It was the 20th century after all and we had answers for things like this: psychosomatic illness, hypnotism, the power of suggestion. But because my friends seemed to believe it, I had a niggling doubt that seeped into my mind, like ink being absorbed into blotting paper. It took one harrowing night to finally convince me.

The reality of curses

I'd been in Alice Springs for about six months helping with the influx of the cyclone refugees. Now this role was coming to an end, I knew I wasn't ready to return home. I relished the freedom in this place and the anonymity that had allowed a daring, somewhat unrestrained side of me to emerge. There was no measuring stick in the form of Anne to keep me moulded in her likeness and so I decided to stay longer and to look for another job.

Quite quickly I found a completely different sort of work at a receiving home for state wards, which was set up mainly because of a growing number of neglected Aboriginal children. Unfortunately the recent introduction of alcohol to a people who for tens of thousands of years had a biology that evolved without it, meant that many had trouble coping with it. Sadly many of them were alcoholics, which affected how they managed their everyday lives. Some of the parents were drunk most of the time and their children suffered. On an average day there were about four babies in the home, but often the numbers could increase to at least ten. It was constant work filling out the files, finding foster homes, and helping out with the day-to-day care of the babies.

"Why the sudden increase in the number of children?" I asked one of the nursing staff as I picked up a howling baby.

"They're clearing the Todd River of all the camps and drunks for the annual boat race."

Thinking she was joking, I laughed. "Oh yeah, right, a boat race in a river without water."

"No, fair dinkum, it's called the Henley on Todd. Tony, the director of this home, has been building his boat for the last few months. A few of us are going in the race with him as his crew. Come on, I'll show you."

Thinking a walk would help settle the baby, I followed her out the back door. We walked down to the end of the yard and there under a tarpaulin was a small boat with a sail.

"I don't get it, is there going to be a sudden downpour to fill the river?"

"No, it only rains enough every few years to get a bit of a flow up. Come here."

As I stepped towards the boat she threw the tarpaulin off and I looked in. The boat had no bottom. Puzzled, I looked up, as she grinned and winked at me.

"So what if our river doesn't have water – a true blue Aussie wouldn't let a little thing like that stop him, would he?"

"What do you mean it wouldn't?" I was feeling irritated that there was so much I didn't know about this place.

"Look, we have to make our own fun out here. Some of the townsfolk spend months designing and building these boats. That's half the fun. There's a competition for the best boat, the most innovative, the craziest etc. Some look like real boats like this one, but others are really imaginative and out there. On the day, the boats, with their captain and crew standing inside, line up in the various categories, and then they run to the finish line. It's such a hoot. You'll have to go. It's on this Sunday."

"I'll go for sure. Trust us Aussies to come up with something like that." "We really are a mad lot, aren't we? We better get back. I'll have to make sure everything's ready for the night staff."

"Oh thanks, that's me. They reckon I'm initiated enough now to handle a night shift."

"You'll be right, and if you get stuck, Tony's right next door. Just hope the babies don't cry all night for you."

"Mmm. Hope so too. Well, at least I have tomorrow off."

By nine o'clock the last of the staff had left and I was alone. Checking everything was securely locked I shut the blinds on the few windows that had them. It was a moonless night, but I could still make out shadowy objects that were unrecognisable in the dark. I wished all the windows had blinds.

A couple of hours later, after I had fed the youngest baby, I walked through the waiting room on my way to the storeroom to get some more nappies. As I switched on the light, something in my peripheral vision made me whisk my head sidewards towards the window. Standing outside was a large Aboriginal woman. Her pale pink floral dress was splattered with stains and covered in red dirt. Her hair was matted, and she leant on a big stick. She squashed her face up against the window and I could see the bloodshot whites of her bulging eyes emphasising the rage in her coal black pupils. She started yelling at me in her native tongue of Pitjantjatjara. As I only knew the odd word, I could not make out what she was saying, but I had a pretty good idea of what she wanted. Without turning around, I stepped backwards towards the counter and pressed the emergency button, thinking that she was going to smash the window with that big stick any minute.

Tony, the director, who lived in the house next door, appeared very promptly. He seemed to know her and he went out the back door and tried to talk to her. She was getting madder and madder and shook her fist at him. In the end he told her that he was going to call the police. At this she started to leave and Tony turned to come inside. As he did, she turned around and pointed at me with the large stick. I could see those eyes, full of rage and determination. She was saying something to herself and trembling all over, but her eyes didn't leave mine.

Tony came in and shut the door. He came over and put a comforting hand on my shoulder, regretting that the incident had happened on my first night duty.

"Sorry you had to have that happen. Poor bugger, she's really pickled her brain, that one. Her baby was the six-month-old boy that the policeman delivered to us yesterday after he found him under a tree in the Todd River. He was badly dehydrated and had a nasty rash on his bottom that was infected. I don't think she'll get him back this time."

"Why?"

"It's the third time we've had this little guy."

"Yeah, I suppose you're right, but I can't imagine any mother would willingly give up her baby."

"If we didn't take him, she'd lose him anyway. He couldn't survive this type of constant neglect. Now forget about this and go and get a bit of rest before the night-time feeds begin. And remember, I'm right next door."

"Sure, but I'm fine. I s'pose I just feel sorry for her."

"We all do, but we need to be pragmatic about it. Good night. Hopefully won't see you 'til morning."

With a big smile he went out. I locked the door after him and headed for the couch to have a nap. I was pretty tired and it did not take long before I fell asleep.

Sometime during the night I awoke to the sound of a baby crying.

"Here we go with the round of feeds," I thought.

I went to open my eyes. They would not open. Then I tried to lift my arms. I couldn't. My legs felt paralysed. I was completely immobilised. It was as if some very strong power was holding me; I just couldn't move. I could hear the baby crying and another one starting to grizzle. I thought perhaps I was still asleep and this was a dream. Giving in to this idea, I relaxed and tried to recapture sleep, yet all I could think about was the Aboriginal woman pointing the large stick at me. I tried to think about something else, but it felt like her eyes of rage were looking at me from the inside of my eyelids. The babies were crying now, louder and more urgently, so again I tried to open my eyes and move, realising that I was awake and not dreaming. I used all my strength to move but I just could not budge. My face felt hot from the effort as I forced every part of my body to break free from whatever was holding me. I don't know how long it went on for, but it must have been quite a while, enough time for most of the babies to be awake, as they were all now howling. I could hear their urgency, which was agitating me more and more.

"Oh my God, what is happening, please help me!" As my thoughts sent this prayer, suddenly I was able to propel myself off the bed. I stood on the floor shaking, heart pounding, breathless. Consciously I took slow breaths in an attempt to relax ... in for five, out for five ... slowly, deeply. As I felt the tension gradually slipping away, I forced myself to put this incident on hold for the time being and deal with the room full of howling, hungry babies. Fortunately this took the rest of the night because it kept my mind off the perplexing incident. At 5.30 am I made a cup of tea and slumped in an armchair to wait for the morning shift. The night's events began to hover in my mind waiting to consume my thoughts as soon as I gave in to them. By 6.30 the staff began to arrive. Soon the kettle was boiling and the smell of coffee and toast came wafting through the building. With the sun rising, the happy chatter among the staff and the comforting smells, the night's events began to diminish in their intensity.

"So you survived the night then, eh?" asked one of the staff, looking at me intently.

"Well ... yes, I did, thanks. Think the littlies all survived," I said trying to sound flippant. Not that she would have any idea of why I looked distracted. She probably thought I found the job too exhausting.

"Mmm, well that's something then, eh? Looks like you better sign off and get home to bed. Off you go. We'll see you the day after tomorrow then, right?"

"Yes. Before I go I just have to write up a bit of an incident we had last night with one of the babies' mother who turned up. Should have done it earlier, but actually I forgot."

"Who was it? It does happen, I'm afraid. It can be very unpleasant. Poor you and on your first night and all."

"I'm OK. It was the mother of the new little boy who was brought in with the bad rash. She was pretty angry, but I buzzed Tony and he came and dealt with her."

"Yes, leave it to him. He can handle them. But this

woman has been here before, and she is a real piece of work. The booze makes her really nasty."

"I reckon a real witch."

I'm sure the nurse took that to mean a bitch, but I knew that this Aboriginal woman was a type of witch who had put a spell on me, just like Marlene had said. A few months later I left Alice Springs, but the memory was not forgotten. Five years later something else would happen that would bring the fearful memories of that night to the surface.

In the ensuing years, my individuality became more defined as I incorporated the parts of myself that emerged through my own experiences and that were different to my sister's. I was feeling more like a whole person, but there was a vacuum inside of me that I attempted to fill in a variety of ways. Finally, after many years, I recognised this vacuum was my spiritual side which I had been aware of but neglected. Surprisingly it turned out to be the most significant part of myself which, when listened and attended to, completed me.

Search for Spiritual Identity

Awakenings

It had been an extremely busy four months after we were born. With tiny baby twins to feed every few hours, my poor mother was extremely tired. Also, my brother began to act out his frustration. He had been an angelic little boy until the day these scrawny crying creatures came into his world, monopolising all the attention that until then had only gone to him. My parents were aware that he felt eclipsed by my sister and me and did all they could to placate him. But the little lad was not quite three and felt he needed to register his protest at having his world turned upside down. So one day he walked into the room where guests were paying homage to these two "usurpers" and poured a bucket of water onto the new carpet.

On the morning of our Christening mother dressed us in beautiful little white dresses made from some of the leftover lace from her wedding gown. The ceremony was to be performed in the same Methodist Church in which my parents had been married a few years earlier.

As they were leaving for the church my mum wearily made a request to my father.

"Can you hold the little one through the Christening please, dear?"

"Of course I'll carry my little Pippen," Dad answered.

He had given me that name because I was so small, only four pounds at birth. "Little pip squeak" was the longer version.

"It's just that she cries all the time and I really don't feel up to handling a crying baby today."

But during the ceremony when the stain of original sin was being removed from our souls and we were being "born of water and the Spirit", I was the one who looked peacefully around the church from over my dad's shoulder while Anne wailed the house down.

Maybe this was an indication of ethereal interests that were to absorb my later life.

When we were nine years old, Mother was walking my sister and me to our piano lesson. It was just an ordinary day like many others, until my sister asked a question.

"What is our purpose for being born? Why do we live at all?"

A moment of epiphany. I felt my soul "quicken". Not that it had been inactive before, but this day it seemed to make itself known to me – much like an infant in the womb is moving from the moment of conception, but the mother only feels it when it reaches a certain size and can touch the edges of her womb. My soul was lightly touching my reason.

I actually do not remember the answer my mother gave to that question. It was the question itself that consumed me from that day on.

Christian roots

Our family continued to attend the Methodist Church until I was about 13 years old. The Methodist branch of Protestant Christianity traces its roots back to 1739 when it developed in England as a result of the teachings of John Wesley. While studying at Oxford, Wesley, his brother Charles, and several other students formed a group devoted to study, prayer and helping the underprivileged. They were labelled "Methodist" by their fellow students because of the way they used "rule" and "method" to go about their religious affairs. Though both the Wesley brothers were ordained ministers of the Church of England, they were barred from speaking at most of its pulpits because of their evangelistic methods. They preached in homes, farmhouses, barns, open fields and wherever they found an audience.

The church buildings were usually plain structures. Inside would be pews, a wooden cross on the wall, choir stalls (the Methodists are renowned for good, hearty singing) and a lectern at which the minister gave his sermon. Once a month we would have communion. This was an activity in which everybody ate pieces of normal bread cut into squares and drank grape juice in individual tiny glasses. By doing this we were continuing to take part in Christ's redeeming resurrection by *symbolically* taking part in His body (the bread) and blood (the juice). They used grape juice instead of wine because Methodists are very against the consumption of alcohol.

The Catholic Church was the new grey building on the corner that our bus passed on the way to school. Back in the 1950s, Protestants would never think of entering a "Mick" church. In fact, as our public school bus from the local primary school pulled up outside the Catholic school to pick the children up, the Protestant children would boo and make condescending jeers towards the "left-footers". One afternoon, when I was still at primary school, I was looking through a children's picture Bible I had received from the Methodist Sunday school. I remember having a strong desire to go to this Catholic Church that I knew always stayed open. So I put a leash on our dog and took her for a walk around the block to the Catholic Church. I tied her up outside at a convenient pole, looked around to see if anyone was about and stole inside.

Attached to the wall, just inside the door was a little bowl of water. I had heard somewhere that this was holy water and that Catholics used it to make the sign of the cross on themselves. I had no idea why they did that, but I thought that this is what you had to do before you entered a Catholic Church. I self-consciously dipped a finger in the water. It felt just like normal water. I smelt it. Nothing. I cautiously put my finger onto my tongue. It just tasted like normal water. I was disappointed. I think I expected it to be different somehow. I very deliberately made the sign of the cross on my chest. I imagined this helped me to get closer to God and I actually felt rather holy at that moment.

I quietly walked inside. There was someone up at the front, kneeling. This was a new idea. We did not kneel in the Methodist Church. I walked down the centre aisle and sat in a seat, far enough away from the "kneeler". I looked around. There was a big cross up on the wall with a dead Jesus hanging on it. We had a smaller cross in the Methodist Church, but it was bare. The only time we ever concentrated on Jesus's death was on Good Friday. I wondered why the Catholics wanted to remember this each time they went to church. I shifted my gaze to a little lantern hanging at the side. It had a soft red glow like a candle was alight inside. That was nice. Around the walls I counted 14 stained-glass windows. They were telling the story of Jesus as he was being judged, carrying his cross and being crucified. There was so much more to see in this church, as if they knew that people needed things to look at as well as to listen to. It would have been good when I was younger, before I could read. I thought it would be much easier to keep my mind on God in here, even if the sermon was boring or I did not understand it.

As I continued to look at these windows, a feeling of great sadness stirred in me at thoughts about what this poor man must have suffered. I averted my gaze to consider the rest of the surroundings. There was a life size statue of a woman on the side. I wondered who she might be. The "kneeler" got up and slid out of the pew. Before she turned to walk up the aisle, she bent down on one knee towards the front of the church. She was bowing to someone like I had seen people bow to the Queen, except there was no one there. Only the little glowing light on the wall.

As she walked past me I asked her, "Excuse me, that statue of the lady. Who is she?"

The lady stopped walking and looked quizzically at me.

"My goodness, don't you know? She is Mary, the mother of Jesus."

"Oh, I see. Thank you."

The woman smiled and then left. I sat in the pew feeling very perplexed. Why have a statue of Mary? The only time I ever heard about her was at Christmas time. I had never thought about her being very important, significant in her role to bear baby Jesus, but that is all. I mean there were plenty of other young Jewish women who could have been his mother. It just happened to be Mary.

I did not know it at that time, but this woman was to exert a great influence on my life many years later.

During my secondary school years, I attended an Anglican all girls' school. Every Tuesday morning for seven years, 300 girls would walk around the corner to a quaint bluestone church where we attended a service. We wore our full school uniform, which included hats and gloves. It was a very different format from the Methodist Church. The only book we used there was a hymn book. This Anglican service had set prayers and readings in a prayer book called The Liturgy and little cushions to kneel on at various intervals. It was all very strange and, I thought, quite old-fashioned and unnecessary. Did anyone really know what it all meant? While the minister with grey hair, long white robes and a really slow voice delivered his sermon, I used to look at the words prominently written on an arch above the altar: "Go ye therefore and teach all nations."

Was it saying that we girls should be doing that? I hoped not.

Our school motto echoed my own leanings. In Latin it was "*Quaerite primo regnum Dei*" which meant "Seek ye first the kingdom of God".

Well, I was not sure if it was God I was looking for, but rather Truth. Maybe it was the same thing, maybe not. As a 14-year-old I was sure it was not to be found in this liturgical old-fashioned church. It seemed particularly old and stuffy to me, who as a teenager was more influenced by all that was happening in the world during the famous 1960s. Existing values were undergoing huge changes. Societal values and beliefs were rebelled against by the "younger generation", spearheaded by the hippy movement, which pushed its love, peace and "flower power" message.

The introduction of "the Pill" freed women to make choices about if and when to choose motherhood and launched the world into "sexual liberation".

The infamous Woodstock music festival in America encapsulated the mood of the time, while anti-Vietnam War rallies challenged the right of the government to be involved.

Following the 1960s Europeans massively abandoned many traditional norms rooted in Christianity and replaced them with continuously evolving relative morality. Moral relativism is the view that ethical standards, morality and positions of right or wrong are culturally based and therefore subject to a person's individual choice. We can all decide what is right for ourselves. Morals and ethics can be altered from one situation, person, or circumstance to the next. Moral relativism makes the claim that it is morally neutral and the concept of right and wrong are not absolute.

I oscillated between feelings of excitement at the bold ideas and intense confusion at being "free" to decide my own moral code.

Samplings of the East

People at the time were beginning to look outside of the established Christian churches to find alternative religious practices which made more sense to them. Many turned to the Eastern religions.

My mother looked into a physical practice that was new in the West. It was yoga. She found a "guru" (teacher) who had come out from India to teach this practice in Australia. He set up a centre and began teaching the physical benefits of yoga exercises and keeping the body flexible. People in the East had been doing these exercises for centuries and they were proven to be very beneficial. He also introduced meditation to calm and focus the mind. This meditation consisted of trying to empty the mind of thought by concentrating on one's breathing and focusing on something inanimate like a lighted candle.

The guru was a very charismatic person with an exotic mystique from a land that none of us had as yet visited. My mother was asked to train as a yoga teacher for the centre. Over the next 15 years, the small centre grew into an institute attracting hundreds of people seeking a novel experience, or meaning for their lives, or inner truth. A number of times a week the guru would hold lectures on how a person could develop him or herself and move along the "eightfold path" towards enlightenment. It required us to look inward to find our faults and weaknesses and then overcome them with much self-effort and determination. Week after week we hung on every word the guru uttered as he explained the path to enlightenment.

Usually Friday night was when the young people attended "the centre", as it was called, to hear the guru. Anne and I began attending these sessions in our final year of secondary school and continued for a couple of years during our tertiary studies. After a long week of school or work, we would rush through peak-hour traffic to be on time. If you walked in late, the guru would glare at you from his little stage built in the corner of the room to elevate him a little above us. He sat on the stage draped in his Indian clothes with his legs crossed in the lotus position informing us of his next piece of wisdom.

One of the attributes our guru emphasised was "serenity". If you were serene then you were evolving well along the eightfold path. We wanted to demonstrate we were evolving so we might attract his attention. This was what we all longed for. So after the rush to arrive on time, about 50 of us would squeeze into a room meant to hold 20. We would sit on the floor with our legs crossed and with quiet determination fix a tranquil look on our faces, as we sat motionless and "peaceful", listening in awe to our guru. He seemed so exotic and full of ancient wisdom. Anne became very involved in the culture of "the centre" and even lived for a while in one of the "yoga" houses which were rented out by young men and women involved in the centre so they could share in a yoga community.

All our family became involved with practising yoga, and also had some individual counselling by the guru.

To begin with I found it fascinating and informative, but gradually alarm bells began to ring. My realisation coincided with the guru's increase in power over the people involved in the yoga centre. He became godlike to his followers who now numbered into the hundreds. Whatever he said went unchallenged and people were following his directions no matter how much they hurt others, their families or themselves. The men began to mimic the guru, by growing beards like his, wearing little hats the same as his and other forms of dress. Their mannerisms so emulated him that individuality morphed into sameness.

One day, many years after my mother had joined the centre, while she was attending the guru's weekly meeting for yoga teachers, he announced that he had dismissed from the centre a couple who had been very dedicated pupils. My mother was incredulous and questioned his decision to dismiss them. By now she had witnessed the heartbreak of many people whose trust and self-respect had been shattered by this man, as well as of a number of the wealthy contributors who had donated most of their money to him, yet now were rejected.

The guru was furious at Mum's challenge. (Anger is a quality that everybody else was supposed to be "working on" to overcome.) This very evolved soul screamed at my mother with flashing eyes and angry gestures, ordering her to leave. With great dignity, Mother slowly rolled up her mat, walked out of the room and the yoga centre for ever. Mother did not return. When her perplexed pupils asked the guru where she was, he responded by telling them she had cancer and had to leave for treatment.

The guru had finally revealed his true self to us.

Nervously we watched as Anne remained emotionally

tied to the guru, willing to do whatever he instructed. This included him telling her to leave the State Education Department and work at the little school he had started. This was going to be a step into more dependency on the guru as it meant working long hours for little pay, with no superannuation or security. It had been proven over the last few years that if for some reason a person dropped out of favour with him, the guru would just tell them to leave without any thought of the consequences.

The other more alarming news was that he had recently given his blessing for a much older man, who was a divorcee, to marry her.

After constant harassing by the whole of our family, we finally pressured Anne into disengaging from the yoga centre. She did not join the guru's school and broke off the relationship with the older man. After a period of time she was relieved she did.

The guru decided to move the yoga centre, including the school, to Queensland and set up behind a certain mountain that he was sure would protect them all from the nuclear fallout when the bombs inevitably came. Many people left jobs, spouses and families to follow him. We heard some years later how numerous individuals and families were severely damaged from this experience.

He always taught us that with the right yoga eye exercises you would never need glasses and with the right mental discipline you could stop your body from getting cancer and other diseases. In time he wore glasses and in his early 70s died from cancer. The experience alerted me to the danger of cults and how easily people can forfeit their personal power into the hands of someone else.

During this time I had the opportunity to visit India with

a girlfriend. She wanted to meet her long-time pen pal from New Delhi and I wanted to catch up with a young Indian woman in Mumbai, whom I had befriended in Australia a number of years earlier. But I particularly wanted to see the guru's country which he had talked so glowingly about. He made India sound mystical and culturally superior to my country. So as an adventurous, naive 22-year-old, I headed to the ancient subcontinent.

Waking up in India

Dilapidated and tired, the rattling train groaned on. I was stiff from a night of lying on a hard board, wedged into a tight space between it and the board above.

"Well, that was the worst night's sleep I've ever attempted," I complained to my travelling companion, Lizbeth, who was sleeping on the board above me. I had tried to get comfortable while encircling my arms around my suitcase to prevent it from getting stolen. I had a crick in my neck and my hip felt bruised from the hard boards. So much for trying to identify with the locals, I thought, as I moaned and said, "Next time we go overnight on a train, we're going first class. Hang the expense."

Glancing opposite I saw the top two boards had been folded against the side of the cabin on their hinges. The bottom bench had been left unfolded to form a seat. Three Sikhs sat side by side, their stained turbans wrapped around their heads like boa constrictors. One had his eyes shut, but the other two were looking at me. I felt conspicuous and a little nervous.

"Lizbeth," I called quietly. "Lizbeth, are you awake?"

After receiving no answer, I bravely rejected the thought of kidnapping and the white slave trade. Lizbeth was tall and slender with fair skin and dark hair, a very attractive combination in India, especially the further south we went. I concluded that she was still asleep after taking more of those potent sleeping tablets her doctor had given her.

There was no use getting up as there would be nowhere to sit, so I lay there and looked around the cabin, trying to avoid eye contact with the men opposite. Curls of mouldy paint hung from the walls, revealing rotting wood. The light fitting was smashed and within was a collection of dead flies and cockroaches that had managed to escape the cobwebs on the ceiling.

I thought back to when Lizbeth and I had planned this trip. Unlike regular tourists, we were going to immerse ourselves in the lives of our Indian friends and their culture. This was the first trip outside of Australia for Lizbeth, and coming from sterile, orderly Canberra, she had reeled with culture shock as soon as we landed in Mumbai (then Bombay). The deprived little bag boys who lugged her big suitcase to the taxi would probably never forget the arrogant white lady.

"I thought they were just being nice," she exclaimed innocently when I tried to explain. "Anyway, I didn't ask them to carry my bags. They just took them as if they were meant to carry them. Drive on, taxi, drive on!" she ordered as the moving taxi forced the child bag carriers to cease clutching the open window waiting for her to throw a few coins.

On arrival at the hotel, Lizbeth, in her best schoolmarm voice, argued with the man behind the reception desk.

"We had confirmation of this room just four hours ago on the plane. I am not leaving this foyer until you give us our room!"

With that she propped herself next to him and glared.

Quietly I slipped him a few rupees and miraculously the room became available.

That was the last comfortable night in over a month. Since then it had been a succession of squalid, cramped and smelly homes. In particular, I dreaded visits to the little room. Over a putrid hole I would crouch in an unstable attempt at the Asian squat. However hard I tried, I always misaimed and hit one or other of my ankles, saturating my sandals. Then carefully, so as not to topple onto the unsanitary concrete floor, I would swivel to the bucket of water next to me, take the cup floating on top, and throw it all over my foot. At other times this was used instead of toilet paper.

The train jolted, bringing my thoughts back to our present situation. The sun was up now, so I knew we would soon be arriving at our next destination. I eased out of the sleeping space and stood on the edge of it to reach Lizbeth.

"Hey, wake up, you," I said, jabbing her in the ribs.

Rolling onto her back, she stretched her long arms as far as she could before the ceiling stopped her.

"Ooo, I'm so stiff," she said yawning. "I might just sleep a little longer."

"No, you won't, we've got to get off this train soon. Oh Lizbeth, I told you not to take those tablets last night. You know they last for eight hours."

"Well, I just couldn't sleep at all on this hard board." She stretched and yawned some more, oblivious to the men opposite watching her.

Presently the train began to screech and shudder as it slowed down. People with trolleys laden with curries, trinkets and cloth lined the platform. A few women in richly coloured saris waited to board the train. Their arms were adorned with gold bracelets nearly up to the elbow, while a ruby or diamond stud gave glamour to the right nostril. Varying sizes of key clusters were clipped to their waists, indicating their wealth to those around. In contrast to their splendour was the drab attire of the majority of women. They had no keys and only a few bangles. They held brooms or balanced washing on their heads and stood away from the other women. It was another indication of the entrenched caste system.

With a loud hiss the train came to a stop. The men opposite smiled their goodbyes as they exited the cabin. As we manoeuvred our cases onto the floor, the cabin window banged open and two beggars hung through, reaching towards us with cupped hands.

I was relieved that they were not deformed beggars.

My first encounter with such a beggar was an experience so shocking that it seared its impression deep into my soul forever. I was sitting in an open rickshaw, a little cart pulled along by a man on a bicycle. Hoping to assist the poor man, who was very skinny and was sweating profusely, I perched on the edge of the seat, imagining that it would make me lighter than if I leant back. Unfortunately this prevented the side of the rickshaw from blocking my view. We pulled up at the side of the road, and I heard someone calling out. I looked down at the pavement to see a pathetic creature tied onto a board with wheels. He was lying on his stomach, his head slightly elongated from the constant strain of looking up. Wasted thighs stuck straight up from his hips, with pieces of shrunken flesh – once healthy calves – dangling from the top. As his hand reached up, I recoiled in horror.

"What happened to him?" I said, gasping.

The rickshaw driver seemed pleased to stop for a moment to catch his breath and offered his explanation.

"He's a pitiful man. Many beggars have found that deformity brings more profit and so they maim some of their children or themselves. The government is trying to ban the practice and encourage people not to give their rupees to them."

"People actually do this to their children?" I cried a little too loudly. I was still looking at the poor man as his cupped hand came towards me. I froze with the shock of it and could not think clearly. I kept staring at him as the reality of what the driver had told me filtered into my mind and heart. I slumped back into the rickshaw disgusted and indignant.

"How could anyone do that to their children? What horrible inhumane people," I lamented.

The rickshaw driver started pedalling again and we continued down the road and away from the beggar. Tears burned the back of my eyes with anger that gave way to guilt. How protected and insular my life had been in comparison. Never once had I gone hungry. If I was an hour or so late with a meal, my stomach would growl and I could get quite irritable, but I never had to worry that I would not satisfy that hunger. But what if I had to live with constant hunger gnawing away at every part of my body and mind? Even worse, what if I had to watch my little children suffer with hunger? Would it finally cause desperation so great that it enabled me to harm my children if I honestly thought it would assist them to get pity money and survive? I would like to think that it would not, but given the same situation as the poor people I had seen were in, I concluded in all honesty that my reasoning could be compromised by such deprivation, and that it might seem like the best thing to do for my child.

As Lizbeth and I dragged our cases to the door of the train, the little beggars hanging through the window disappeared, only to be found standing at the doorway, hands outstretched as we tried to exit. I dreaded these guilt-ridden moments. My pity instincts battled with the advice my friend Shernaz had given us when we'd arrived in India.

"You have to understand something about the beggars," she explained. "If we Indians give money to the beggar, they will know that this person's karma has been met, as it is only required to give to the poor once a day. Therefore they will not expect any more money to be given by them. But if they see a foreigner giving money, they assume this person feels pity and soon this person, whom they perceive to be very wealthy, is rushed by hundreds of beggars. Many of these people could get work, but they choose to beg instead. So I suggest you refuse to give to them. I would say to them, *'kum karu'*, which means 'do work'."

Easing our way out of the train, I avoided looking into the eyes of the boy beggars, and said in as firm a voice as I could muster through my guilt, *"Kum karu."*

Lizbeth was still in a sleeping-drug stupor, so I grabbed her with my spare hand and pulled her down the platform through more beggars, trinket sellers and bag boys.

Standing outside the station, I scanned the surroundings until I spotted men riding their rickshaws around and around, waiting for customers. Holding an arm up in the air I yelled, "Rickshaw!"

About 20 rickshaw drivers eagerly pedalled at top speed towards us. They formed a circle around us, shouting and waving their hands, trying to be the one we chose. I felt like a tiny fish about to be enclosed in a sea anemone.

Dazed and slightly alarmed, I struggled to remember

where we were going. One of the rickshaw men grabbed my arm saying, "Where you want to go, memsahib?"

"Just a minute …" I fossicked in my bag feeling more and more anxious as they continued to yell at us, each one trying to get our business. "Here it is. We are meeting some people at The Grand Hotel. Can you take us there please?"

"*Achar*," he said, rocking his head from side to side which resembles a "no" to me, but which goes with a "yes" in India.

Pushing myself through the man circle, I grabbed Lizbeth, who had been watching the proceedings with the glazed smile of a person in the middle of a pleasant dream. I shoved her into the rickshaw and went to climb in after her.

"Oh no, memsahib. You both cannot ride in this. You will need two 'taxis' with those big cases."

He half pulled me off, while he signalled to his relative who had been lurking nearby. I expected to see a car taxi, but realised as his relative pedalled over that the "taxi" was his humble bike and cart.

Finally we set off. I was still feeling hassled and somewhat irritated by the arrogance I felt from the driver. The bitumen road narrowed, becoming a dusty track, and shops became more like tents than buildings. It occurred to me that we were heading out of town.

"Hey, driver, I was told The Grand was in the middle of town. Where are we going?"

"The Grand is not so good, memsahib. I know of a much better hotel," he said as he puffed and began to pedal harder.

"But we have arranged to meet some friends. Please, take me back!"

"No, no, memsahib, you will like this place much better.

My uncle runs it and it's very nice. We are nearly there." He kept riding, ignoring my pleas to turn around.

Panic was threatening to overtake me and I looked back at Lizbeth, seeking a visual exchange of encouragement. But her face was glazed with a blissful amnesia. Sinking back in the seat I felt utterly insignificant and vulnerable in this massive country, where all around people struggled to merely survive. I pressed my suitcase close to my chest, like a child hugging a security blanket. It contained only a fraction of my possessions and I acknowledged with shame that it contained more wealth than many people here would ever have. As that thought germinated, I sat up with a jolt.

Here we were, two young Western women, hijacked by these rickshaw men, and we were being taken out into the middle of nowhere. Nobody at home knew exactly where we were. Any minute we could be murdered and robbed. We could disappear forever!

"Now look here," I yelled. "You turn around now, right now, do you hear me?"

Ignoring his slightly hysterical passenger, he kept pedalling for what seemed like a long time. My constant entreaties, increasing in volume and pitch, fell on deaf ears.

Finally he pulled up outside a red brick building with a broken window.

"Majestic Manor" the boldly hand-painted sign jeered as it hung precariously on its rusted hinges.

My knees were shaking as I stepped onto the ground. In a few quick lunges I was beside Lizbeth's rickshaw, urging her to come down. I signalled to another rickshaw, as a number of them were nearby.

"Memsahib, what are you doing? You have not seen this fine hotel. Come, come, follow me and have a look."

There was no way we were going to stay there, but I was already too shaken and intimidated by this man to ignore him. As we entered the building, the driver greeted the proprietor with great enthusiasm and familiarity. We took a quick walk up the hall, which was as dilapidated as the outside, and then with exaggerated determination we walked out to a group of rickshaw drivers that had gathered.

With my voice sounding an octave higher, I demanded, "Will you take us immediately to The Grand Hotel back in town?"

Just as we had got into two new rickshaws, the other driver, who had followed us out of the hotel, started yelling and waving his arms around.

"Come on, driver, please. I want you to get going NOW!"

"Memsahib, this man says that you have not paid him."

"Well, no, because he didn't take us where we asked him to. Come on, please, just get us out of here."

More yelling and more frantic gesturing.

"I'm sorry, memsahib, but you must pay."

By now Lizbeth had finally woken up properly and realised our predicament. We both dived into our purses and handed the money over.

It was nearly noon when we finally arrived at The Grand Hotel. As Lizbeth and I later relaxed on the veranda with our cool drinks, looking out at the lush, well-tended gardens, we realised we had been very lucky to end up safely back at this hotel. We hoped we were now a little wiser about how to manage rickshaw drivers.

On our return to Mumbai I caught up again with my friend Shernaz. She was taking us to her home to stay for a couple of nights and to meet her parents. The taxi had stopped at a small intersection. Women in brightly coloured saris, sellers with their carts and groups of chattering teens straggled across the road. An old man caught my attention. He was dressed in the typical wide trousers and long white top. A tattered grey woollen vest was pulled over it all, probably to add some warmth. His long hair and beard matched his clothes and he was standing at the edge of the road as everybody pushed past him. I was wondering if he was attempting to cross when suddenly he collapsed into the gutter. Nobody stopped to help. They just walked around him. Grabbing the door knob of the taxi, I was about to jump out when Shernaz stopped me.

"That poor old man! He's just collapsed and nobody is helping him. We better do something," I yelled.

"It's OK, his family will come," she replied.

The taxi took off and I kept looking back.

"Shernaz, he is still lying there! Everybody is walking past him."

"Well," she answered, "this is his karma. It is not our business to interfere."[1]

Although India was a fascinating ancient country full of bright colours and delicious food, a number of things bothered me. This experience of the old man seared into my heart as did some other observations.

Although efforts had been made to abolish it, the caste system was very much alive. It appeared to trap people in the level of society they were born into with little flexibility to ever move. At the top of the five castes was the Brahman. If you were lucky enough to be born into this highest caste, it meant you were being blessed from the goodness of your

---

[1] In Hinduism, karma refers to the totality of a person's actions and reactions in this and previous lives, all of which determines the future. Example: if one sows goodness, one will reap goodness. If one sows evil, one will reap evil.

past lives and were therefore entitled to be above the other castes. You enjoyed money, status and privilege.

At the other end of the caste system were the "harijans", the untouchables. If you were born into this caste it was believed that you deserved it due to the bad things you had done in your past life. The harijans lived in slums and undertook the most menial dirty jobs that no one else would ever do. None of the other castes would have anything to do with them.

One afternoon I was in a rickshaw being pedalled along by a skinny little man with sweat pouring off his taut, overused body. I knew I was giving him money for his hard work, but it still seemed like he was more of a beast of burden than a human being. As he pedalled away, I unintentionally found myself comparing my Western culture with what I was observing here in India. One aspect that I was considering was the human dignity of each individual and how it appeared to be different in this country. Like a butterfly hovering over a flower until it is ready to settle, a thought was hovering around my mind trying to enter my consciousness. Gently the thought landed as I came to a conclusion. It appeared to me that of all the religions I had so far experienced or read about, it was Christianity which emphasised the infinite dignity of each individual person. Stories I had heard as a young child in Sunday school marched across my mind one after another. The one about the lost sheep that had wandered away from the fold and the good shepherd who was desperate to find this one little sheep and left the rest of the flock to search for it.[2] There were many Bible stories about the rejected and despised

---

2   Luke 15.

people in society whom Jesus had befriended and helped.[3] He did not judge or blame them for what they had done, but reached out to them with healing and forgiveness, eager to release each person from any sort of bondage or sickness. This religion, I realised, freed people from the harshness of reincarnation that holds them in bondage to past lives from which they cannot escape. This attitude would prevent them from improving their life and developing to their full potential.

As this thought germinated, another image came to mind of a wrinkled face encircled by a blue and white veil. It was the face of a Catholic nun, Mother Teresa, who had been on the cover of a book I had read some time ago. She had devoted her life to helping the poor in Calcutta (now Kolkata). I remembered being touched by the attitude she had to all people, especially to the ones that society had rejected. As I recall, she had taken quite literally the words of Jesus:

"I was hungry and you fed me. I was naked and you clothed me. I was sick and you consoled me ... as you did it to one of the least of these my brethren, you did it to me."[4]

She worked in particular with dying people who were abandoned, the poorest of the poor. I am sure she would have stopped to help the man who had collapsed in the gutter because he was of immense value, despite the life he lived. Mother Teresa took all people in, cared for them and showed them love. She gave many of them a dignity in their death that they had never experienced before in life.

"She did not evangelise the gospel in the propagandist sense. She preached Christ every moment of every day by living for Him

---

3   Matthew 18-19, Luke 15:1-10, Mark 2:13-15, John 8:3-11.
4   Matthew 25.

and in Him," observed Malcolm Muggeridge in his book *Something beautiful for God*.

The selflessness and faith of this woman was the antithesis to what I had experienced within the yoga centre. She did not judge a person as being a less evolved soul or inferior to her because they were poor, ill or non-Christian. She loved and served them unconditionally. I had been impressed by this woman when I read about her. But now I was actually in India, experiencing the inescapable poverty, the crowded chaotic streets, the dirt and heat, my admiration for her had grown exponentially. Mother Teresa was physically a small woman who had chosen to live and work among the unloved and forsaken people. I wanted to know where she found the strength, courage and humility to do this work.

For two months Lizbeth and I visited many places in India, from the Asian Plateau of Panchgani to remote villages where people lived dependent on the monsoon rain for their crops. The warmth and generous hospitality of the people wherever we went was humbling, especially in the rural villages. In those places we felt like we had gone back in time to an ancient way of life that still persisted today.

We travelled to one of these villages out in the countryside on a bullock wagon that swayed from side to side as the bullock lumbered along the dirt track. At one stage a red truck came roaring along the same path towards us and the poor bullock took fright and pulled us into a ditch. The driver started yelling and hitting its hide with a thin pole, but the bullock was not in any hurry, preferring to nibble on a bit of grass. The driver signalled for us to get out of the wagon whereupon he began to pull the creature by the yoke around its neck to get it back on the path. Finally we were on our way and presently came upon a cluster of about five houses encircled by a brick wall.

Just before we drove through the gate in the wall, the driver stopped to talk to a group of women who were squatting outside the wall mixing cow dung with water and patting it into rounds between their hands. Then they proceeded to slam the dung "patties" onto the brick wall to dry. This was what they used for fuel on their cooking fires. With the scarcity of trees around, it was obvious they needed to find alternative fuel sources. When we drove through the gate a few people came up to greet us, but my attention was drawn to another group of women squatting together near a flat pan on a little open fire. The women were mixing and patting the dough for the naan bread in the same manner as they made the dung patties, but instead of putting them on the wall they placed them onto the pan.

The family we were visiting in this village asked us into their house for a meal. It was a very humble home with a dirt floor, devoid of any windows, which made it quite dark. Obviously this helped to keep the house cool in the ferocious heat of summer. The wife began mixing up some naan dough in a metal bowl while the elder daughter collected some cups from a makeshift shelf in the corner of their one-room dwelling. The husband ushered us to a woven mat on the floor where we waited for the kettle to boil. He sat with his legs tucked under him, smiling at us – the universal language between people when they can't understand words. We smiled back, although we felt embarrassed at all the fuss they were going to for us. But offering food to guests is a worldwide custom of hospitality, and even in their poverty they were willing to share with us. I left feeling so humbled by their generosity and also with a deep sense of guilt at the standard of living I took for granted in Australia without appreciating how privileged I was.

One afternoon in Mumbai, I stood outside the "The Mother House". This was the home and yoga centre of the guru's parents. The guru had often talked about this place and about his parents, who he assured us were very "evolved" souls. From all he had told us I expected it to be a large, important-looking building. But it was a very ordinary, medium-sized dwelling with an untended small garden enclosed by an innocuous wire fence. It was difficult to imagine that someone who yielded such influence over thousands of people came from such a humble dwelling.

I had fantasised about this moment many times back in Australia. I imagined myself storming into this house to expose the truth about their son to his parents, telling them how he had ruined people's lives and hurt many others. I wanted to tell them that we had all trusted him and believed the things he told us about spiritual enlightenment and how yoga helps this to happen. I wanted to diminish him in the eyes of the two people he loved and admired so much.

I stood there pondering all these memories for half an hour. The small gate to enter their property was right in front of me. But the experiences in this country over the last couple of months had changed me. Revenge on the guru seemed unimportant now. There was something else much more pressing making its presence felt. I did not immediately recognise it but it felt like an immense empty void within the centre of my being. Over the ensuing years I tried to fill that void in a variety of ways. It was only much later that I identified that feeling as a spiritual hunger.

Slippery slope

On my return to Australia I continued to develop my new career as an orientation and mobility instructor. This was teaching blind people how to orientate themselves through their dark world using white cane techniques and other methods to organise their daily living.

But spiritually I felt blind. The pulls of the world and many inner conflicts drove me in directions that depleted and wounded me. In an attempt to fill this void in my life I had even become engaged to a man who I realised was not right for me. I had all the engagement presents from the big party and wore his ring, but I was empty and emotionally worn out. It was not that I did not love him anymore; it was more the realisation that I had never loved him. On the surface he met all the requirements of a "good catch" – very tall and good-looking, with a promising career, from a solid background similar to my own, and he loved me.

I had actually met him during my trip to India, in the southernmost point, a town called Cochin. It was known for the place where Saint Thomas landed on his missionary outreach to India during the first century. The people in this town were quite small and dark skinned compared with the fairer, taller people I had been staying with in northern India. That's why I had easily noticed a very tall man crossing the road coming towards me. His first words were, "You look like the right colour!"

It was a humorous beginning to our friendship. He was completing a five-year stay in England by travelling over land with a couple of friends in a campervan. Eight months after I met him, he arrived back in Australia and contacted me where he knew I was working.

Being with him plunged me into a lifestyle to which I was unaccustomed. He was liked by everyone and had countless friends and female admirers. His social life was a whirl of parties, dinners and get-togethers. Initially I thought it was fun and exciting to have so many things to do and many new people to get to know. But after a while it began to frustrate me. I found the conversations repetitive and superficial, accentuating the emptiness I felt. Yet, another wounded part of me was flattered that this good-looking, popular man loved me, and so when he proposed, I accepted.

It was only after the big engagement party and when the date and venue for the wedding had been set that the finality of our relationship began to deeply unsettle me. I wrestled with my conscience for a number of weeks as I admitted to myself that I could not spend the rest of my life with him.

At this particularly confusing, empty time in my life a man from the distant past reached across the centuries with a message.

"You have made us for Thyself, O Lord, And our hearts are restless until they rest in Thee."

He was a Catholic bishop from the fourth century, Saint Augustine. These words profoundly touched the emptiness that I had been experiencing for many years and with an immediate epiphany I realised that what had been crying out was my starving soul. Even the thought that my soul needed attention gave me a small sense of peace and from that feeling grew the desire to pursue this neglected part of myself. In fact, I did not see how I could continue with my life until I did. This, I knew, was going to take time, so I asked for three months off work and postponed the wedding, assuming that I would have it all figured out by then.

I felt I was suffocating with all the intense conflicting emotions and my heart was sagging with sadness. I just wanted to run away from everything for a while.

Seek and you will find

During my early teens our family had been introduced to an international organisation called Initiatives of Change (IOC). The people involved emphasised the reconciliation of world conflicts. The ideology was based on the premise that there would never be peace in the world while individuals continued to live selfish, dishonest lives. They believed that by recognising these inner faults and with the help of a higher power human nature could change. This power was from whichever source made most sense to a person's religion and culture.

I had met many people within IOC and they appeared to live with purpose and faith. So it was to this organisation that I turned when I began my spiritual search. At this time Anne had taken a year out from her teaching career to spend a year in Sweden with a young woman who worked in this organisation. So Anne was immersed in working with IOC in Sweden and Lapland. But I longed to see an elderly couple who had become friends with my family through IOC. They lived in Sussex, England.

Janice was an outgoing American from one of the wealthy establishment families of New York, the Van Dykes. She had been brought up surrounded by sophistication, parties and money and had decided there was more to life than what she had experienced and so joined IOC where she met her husband, James. He was a reserved English gentleman, an Oxford Dean, playwright and an Anglican clergyman. For years an invitation had been offered to any of our family to visit. So one by one each member of the family had gone to stay with them and now it was my turn. It had been ten years since I had seen them. Back then I had been enthusiastic about life and full of hope.

Arriving back in the land of my ancestral roots was exciting. As I travelled on the train from London Airport to Sussex, I thought about my great-great-grandparents, who as a young couple had made the six-month trip by boat out to Australia in 1870.

They were about my age when they undertook that arduous journey, but tragically the new country greeted them with sorrow. The day after they landed, their little baby died. It was a story that I had heard a number of times, a story that challenged me. This couple had arrived in Australia with very little money and they needed to bury their baby. An offer was made to have their child buried for free in a pauper's grave or they could pay for a Christian burial. With their last sovereign they paid for the baby to be given a Christian burial.

I had often thought about this choice and wondered if I agreed with the decision. What did he and his wife eat and where did they live without money? What was so important about a Christian burial? *It was this very question that was about to be answered during my time in England.* The most amazing end to this story was that this man became very wealthy and held a number of important positions in his community as well as being a secret philanthropist. When he died, most of the town of Horsham in Victoria turned out to his funeral and only then did it become apparent how much he had done over the years for people in need.

As the train pulled up at the station in Sussex, I could see Janice and James waiting for me. After fond greetings, they drove me to their home which was a little way out of town. The pretty cottage was set amidst a large garden abloom with summer annuals. A variety of rose bushes dominated one corner while bright blue delphiniums lined the path. Spilling out of numerous garden beds were nasturtiums and zinnias, while a sweet smelling creeper grew over an arch near the front door. Before we went inside I marvelled at the huge bumble bees that were meandering among the flowers.

Inside, the cottage was elegantly decorated with polished wooden furniture, various paintings and ornaments from the couple's travels, and bowls of fresh flowers on the table and chiffonier – a cosy atmosphere in which to relax with my old friends. Presently we settled down to dinner at the table set with fine china. The silver cruet set had a small salt container with its own tiny spoon and the crystal tumblers tinkled as iced water was poured into them from the etched glass pitcher. I felt very honoured to be welcomed with such grace. I observed these two dear friends with affection. As James talked, his head wobbled slightly as if his neck was struggling to hold his head upright. I had forgotten that about him. It was a unique idiosyncrasy that portrayed a vulnerability which I found endearing. They had been devoted to each other for nearly 40 years, travelling the world to put on his plays and support the organisation they believed in.

By about eight o'clock, jet lag gripped me and reluctantly I left the enjoyable gathering and headed for bed. The delightful attic bedroom had double-hung windows with cochineal pink floral curtains trimmed with plain burgundy. The chair, at an angle in the corner, had been covered with the same fabric, as had the dressing table. In the soft light of the bedside lamp it could have been a room out of a decorating magazine, advertising a typical English bedroom. Earlier in the day I had gazed out the window to a view of rolling green fields quite different to the landscape of home. It was greener with a softer light and hedges instead of fences. Dots of white sheep punctuated the hillside that sloped gently into the valley. Amidst this peaceful setting I nestled beneath the blankets and sleep engulfed me immediately.

I do not know how long it had been but I was woken by the sounds of footsteps. I thought that perhaps I had only slept for a short while and that it was James and Janice heading off to bed. I turned over wanting to go back to sleep. More footsteps. They seemed to be in my room so I switched on the light. Nobody there. I looked at my watch – 12.30. Creeping out of bed I opened the door a little to see who was still up. The house was in darkness. I stood in the hallway near the stairwell to hear if anybody was awake downstairs. No lights were on and all was quiet.

Puzzled, I got back into bed. I sat there for a few minutes listening, and then lay down and switched the light off. Sleep was on its way when I heard the footsteps again. This time I was sure they were in my room. Nearly knocking the lamp off the bedside table, I managed to switch it on, anxiously wondering who on earth would be in my room at this time of night. There was nobody, just sounds that I thought were footsteps. But obviously I had been wrong, there was nobody there. I kept the light on and listened. There they were again. Was there an animal walking around on the roof? I had heard possums back home and they clumped along sounding something like this. As there were no possums in England I assumed there was something like an English possum equivalent having a nocturnal stroll on the roof. I turned the light off again and expected to fall off to sleep pretty quickly, as I was exhausted from the long flight.

But as I lay there I could not ignore the sounds. I felt quite sure they were not coming from outside the room and they were certainly not outside on the roof. They were inside the room and close to my bed. I sensed a presence. The pounding in my head must have been from my heart, but it sounded like African drums signalling danger. I took little breaths of air as if this would help me to be silent and invisible. I could not swallow or move and felt perspiration seeping out along my backbone. This noise was all around me. There was someone walking around the room, there was no mistaking it. They were as close as they could get to me without jumping on the bed. With this alarming thought I pulled the lamp onto the bed and switched the light on. I sat clutching the lamp as if it were a weapon. The room was empty even though I could still hear the footsteps.

After sitting for quite a while peering into the room, I placed the lamp back on the bedside table and lay on my back with the blankets clutched tightly under my chin. For the remainder of the night I lay there listening, looking, drifting in and out of sleep. Even though I could see no one, someone was there and they were letting me know it.

As soon as morning came and I could hear James and Janice heading downstairs, I quickly dressed and went down to breakfast. Janice was putting a tea-cosy on the freshly made pot of tea while James placed the toast into a silver toast rack. Little bowls of marmalade and blackberry jam were placed on the white linen tablecloth. Boiled eggs in china egg cups with the same floral design as the breakfast china were positioned in front of each setting alongside which were linen serviettes folded through silver rings.

"Good morning, dear. Come and sit here and help yourself. Like a cup of tea?"

"Yes, please, Janice. Nice and strong."

James stopped chopping the top off his egg and stood until I was seated.

"I think a strong cup is in order for her, my dear. You still look very tired. Did you sleep well?"

My head was feeling very foggy as I debated with myself if I should tell them. The hope was that they could offer an explanation. The risk was that they might think I was crazy. During the following years I would need to make this decision many times, whom to trust with this experience and whom I should not.

This morning was the first time that I decided to risk it and trust the elderly couple.

"Well, I did and I didn't sleep well. I mean I crashed when my head hit the pillow." Taking a sip of tea, I paused longer than a normal interlude, while I outlined in my head the gist of what I was about to say.

They sipped their tea, waiting for me to continue.

"Look, I can't really explain it. I know you'll think I'm crazy, but I had been asleep and a noise woke me." I proceeded to tell them about my night experiences. I saw them exchange glances, which flustered me, but I had to keep going to finish the story.

"I kept the light on all night, but didn't see anyone."

Janice stirred sugar in her tea while James looked

sympathetically at me, his head gently wobbling. I felt they were not quite sure how to respond. So after what seemed like quite a while I asked, "Do you believe in evil spirits?"

"Yes, I do," James responded. "But why do you want to know about evil spirits?"

"I had an experience about five years ago when an old Aboriginal lady cursed me. Until then, I thought it was all primitive mumbo jumbo but after that I really think there is some spooky stuff around."

James sipped his tea and placed the cup deliberately into the saucer.

"Well, yes, I do believe in evil spirits." The wobbling of his head became more pronounced. "But I'm sure you imagined it all because you were very tired last night and also you had been through a stressful time before you left Australia. It's such a very long flight. You were more than likely quite jet-lagged. Why don't you try and relax today. Go for a walk in the fields and get some fresh air."

I felt my face flushing as I thought hard to find a flippant remark to divert any assumptions that I was "not quite right".

"Of course. Jet lag is a rotten thing. I'd forgotten how badly it affects me."

With that everybody seemed satisfied. We resumed drinking tea and piling homemade marmalade onto toast as we chatted away about everyday matters. James, being a writer, was such a good storyteller. He began a tale about his gardener who was born and raised in the heart of the woods and knew the plants and animals of the territory within easy reach of his home intimately. He called himself the "three mile man". James thought of using that description as the title of his new book.

In the light of day, sitting in the cosy kitchen beyond which I could see the lovely green fields, the scary events from the night began to diminish in my mind until I decided that it must have been something like a bad dream.

Hope in a horse trough

After breakfast I decided a walk in the garden would help refresh me. I also wanted to ponder how I should go about finding God and walking helped me to think.

Strolling over to the side fence I noticed a horse trough filled with water, although there were no longer any horses on the property. With horror I saw that a little bird had fallen in. Its wings were outstretched and its limp head was face down in the water. It had obviously fallen in while taking a drink, and could not fly out with its wet wings. Sadness and a surge of hopelessness wafted through me. Then a slight flutter of its wings sent ripples through the water.

"Oh, you poor little thing, you are still alive," I said, gasping, as I plunged my hand into the trough and scooped out the sodden feathery bundle.

"Janice, Janice! Have you got an old box?" I yelled as I ran inside and then stood on the tiled kitchen floor, the dripping water from the bird forming a puddle around my feet.

"Oh my goodness, let's see now. Yes, I have a small cardboard box that I store material scraps in."

With that Janice went to the cupboard, found the box and tipped the fabric scraps out onto the table.

"Here we are and here is a soft piece of flannel that you

can use to lay it on. It's probably cold. Why don't we place it in front of a heater for a while to dry it out?"

For the rest of the day the bird lay on its side with its eyes shut except for when I tried to force-feed it some warm porridge. Then it flicked them open and shut like a camera lens. At bedtime James suggested I put the bird in the garden shed for the night. I think we all realised it was going to die.

The next morning as I headed downstairs I could hear James talking to a man who sounded very enthusiastic about something.

"Well, well, here she is. Come over here, our gardener wants to meet you."

At the open back door stood a man in a brown flannel shirt over which was a dark blue anorak. On his head was a checked woollen cap, the sort a country squire might wear. He was clean shaven and had the ruddiest cheeks I had ever seen. He raised his cap as a greeting.

"How d'ya do, ma'am," he said, while looking down at his muddy boots.

"Fine, thanks. You?"

"Oh, 'tis a good morning, that's to be sure. So you're the one then that rescued the woodpecker?"

"Rescued? Oh, the little drowned bird. So it's a woodpecker. Did it survive the night then?"

"Oh yes, to be sure. When I opened the shed this mornin' it was sitting on the bench. I saw at once that it was a Lesser Spotted. A rare find, been trying for years to photograph one. So I got a picture before I let it go. It flew to the top of the ash, looked around to find its bearings, let out a short burst of sound and was off. I shall look out for it again. Lesser Spotteds like apple trees, so you might find them more around the garden than in the woods. Well, better get on with the work now. Half the morning's nearly gone. Good day to you, miss."

With that he touched the tip of his cap and headed off into the garden.

"He's quite a reserved man," said James. "But this morning was the first time I've ever seen him animated over anything. He's a serious birdwatcher, you see, and this morning when he opened the garden shed and saw the rare woodpecker, he was so excited. He borrowed my camera to get a photo of it before he set it free. It's a good thing that you saved such a rare bird."

"So our little drowned bird is very rare and I saved it." As this thought enfolded me, I felt like I had received a warm kiss from Heaven and hope seeped into my soul.

Nocturnal visitor returns

I spent the rest of the day picking blackberries and walking around the green fields near the cottage. After another nice dinner, which included my fresh blackberries, we all headed off to bed. Sometime during the night somebody tapped me on the shoulder. It woke me up. In those first dreamy moments I thought I was back home and that my sister was trying to wake me. As I turned over to face her I might have said something like, "Oh, Anne, what is it now?"

Then I snapped awake as I realised where I was. This time I knew that everybody was asleep. I lay there hardly able to breathe, listening to the footsteps that moved all over the floor of my room. There was someone there and it was like they wanted me to know it. It sounded like someone was walking up the walls and even along the ceiling.

My temples throbbed as I shivered within my clammy skin. This time I was too scared to even reach out for the light. I lay there hour after hour with the blankets gripped tightly under my chin, drifting between sleep and alertness. Finally the birds started signalling the morning, but I didn't move until the sunlight had brightened the room.

I wondered what I should do. Should I bring up the

subject again over breakfast? Even if I did, I had no tangible evidence, just another night filled with footsteps and now a tap on the shoulder. Anyway, how can you explain things invisible? You cannot see the wind, but you can see its effect on the trees and the leaves blowing along the ground. The same with electricity – until you see the globe light up you would not know it is there. But with this presence I could not point to moving leaves or a light globe so I decided to keep quiet. I would try and ignore it and enjoy the remaining time with my dear old friends.

    I stayed with James and Janice for about two weeks and then was invited to stay in a London home at the salubrious address of Charles Street. This was another house that had been donated to the work of Initiatives of Change. It was just down the street from Berkeley Square. This beautiful four-storey home was decorated with expensive furniture and entertained influential people, including diplomats and politicians from all over the world. I helped out in the kitchen and waited at the table during some of the dinner meetings. The kitchen was in the basement so there was a little food lift that took meals up to the first floor dining room. There were also chutes on each floor that sent your dirty washing to the laundry.

    My bedroom was on the fourth floor, which was accessible by trusting a very old lift. I'm sure it was kept in good repair but it was jerky and prone to getting stuck between floors. I shared the room with a French girl, Natalie, who laughed at everything. I felt she brightened up the rather stiff English household.

    Most nights since I had left Sussex, I had been woken up by a tap on my shoulder or footsteps around the room. One night I had been woken as usual and was trying to ignore the noise as I did most nights, when Natalie quietly got out of bed to visit the bathroom. When she returned I asked her if she could hear anything unusual in the room.

She was silent for a moment and then said, "*Non, mon amie*. Just the noisy traffic from the square. I think I will close this window and see if it will shut some of it out."

"So ... ah, um ... you can't hear anything like someone walking around our room?"

"What, you mean like someone is hiding here, going to jump on our beds and try and frighten us? We know you're here, whoever it is, just ..."

"No, no. There's no one in here. I'm just rambling on. Let's go back to sleep. Good night, *bonsoir*."

After staying in this house for about a month I was invited to stay at the organisation's estate in Tarporley near Chester. The magnificent stately home, set on ten acres of land, was called Tirley Garth. The long drive up to the house was lined with huge rhododendron trees that exploded into masses of colour during the spring. The rest of the garden contained ponds with water lilies, a croquet lawn, a tennis court, terraced gardens and a big fountain splendidly placed in the centre of the circular driveway at the front of the house. During the time I lived there I enjoyed watching the garden undergo its seasonal changes, each holding its own particular beauty. The garden had obviously been planned with this in mind – something beautiful to look at all through the year.

At Tirley Garth I shared a room with a young German woman, Greta. She was a physiotherapist back home and was taking some time out of her career to work voluntarily with the organisation. Initially I thought she was rather a serious person with that clipped accent and precise ways representative of her nationality. But after we had roomed for a while I realised she was very warm with a great sense of humour. Her last name was Schmitt-Gerka, which I thought sounded like gherkin, so this became her nickname. A familiar gesture such as a special name can help glue a friendship. It was a friendship that I needed at this time and I was relieved to be sharing with her. Even though nobody else, it seemed, could hear the footsteps, it was comforting to know I was not in the room alone. I was especially glad in the following weeks because my nocturnal visitor was getting impatient.

In the middle of one night, after a tap on my shoulder I heard a great gasp from underneath my pillow.

"Oh my gosh, what was that?" I screamed, propelling myself out of bed. I stood shivering in the middle of the room.

"What was what?" said Gherkin, turning on the light. "What's wrong, have you had a bad dream?"

After months of enduring fearful nights and disturbed sleep I needed to tell someone what was going on and I felt Gherkin would not dismiss me as crazy. Anyway, I had to take the risk. I sat on the side of her bed, wrapped in a blanket, and told her what had been going on.

"Well, I don't know vot is happening, but God does. Let's ask Him to show you and protect you."

At that we knelt by her bed and she prayed. I cried silently as my shaking body began to grow calmer.

Each night Gherkin and I would pray. I also tried lying up the other way in my bed and even found a new pillow. I suspected this would not change anything, but at least I was doing something.

A few nights later I woke to hear scratching noises

coming from the cupboard. Initially I thought it was an animal trapped inside that was trying to get out.

"Gherkin, ... are you awake?"

"Mmm."

"Can you hear that noise coming from the cupboard?"

"Mmm? Vot noise?"

"The scratching noise. Do you think it might be a rat in there?"

"I can't hear anything," she answered through a big yawn.

"You sure? It sounds like claws on the wood."

"Mmm. No. Nothing. It's very late. Good night."

"Night, Gherkin. Sorry to wake you."

The cupboard was right next to my bedhead but it was only a small room and the noise was quite loud. If she could not hear it, then it had to be my "visitor". I lay still and listened carefully, trying to calm my thumping heart, which was so loud in my ears that it threatened to mask the sound. Before too long I felt I had identified the cause. It was the sound of fingernails scraping down the cupboard door.

Ray of light

Three months had passed since I'd arrived in England, and for most of that time I had been working voluntarily with the Initiatives of Change organisation. This organisation was well known for its professional musicals and play productions, many of which travelled worldwide spreading the message of honesty and reconciliation between individuals and nations. Sometimes the plays were about inspirational people. One of the producers, Gerard, asked me if I would like to join the cast of a play that was travelling throughout the United Kingdom.

"This play is about a man called Keir Hardy. Have you heard of him?"

"No, I haven't. Who is he?"

"I suppose he was better known here in the United Kingdom than in Australia. He was an early 19th century Scottish parliamentarian who began the trade union movement for coalminers in Wales."

"They used to have a pretty awful time of it, didn't they?"

"Did they ever! The mines were extremely unsafe. Most of the ones in Wales were owned by wealthy English companies that kept the running costs down by neglecting health and safety."

"Really! That's inexcusable. Maybe they should have been put down a mine for a day!"

Gerard smiled and nodded at this as he ushered me to a seat in the lounge room where a tray of tea and biscuits had been placed on the side table. As he sat in the armchair it was obvious that he wanted me to pour the tea as he continued our conversation.

"Actually, on an earlier tour, the cast was invited to go down a mine just out of Cardiff. Of course, they're nothing like they used to be. All the modern safety gear and monitoring systems are there now and they have electric lights, rather than dingy little lamps. And the tunnelling is secure. But even so, I was pleased to get out of there, and that was the sentiment of most of the cast."

"I reckon I'd be the same. Two jobs I don't think I could ever do would be a miner or working on a submarine. I'd be so scared that something would go wrong and I'd be stuck in a dark confined space where the limited air would inevitably run out. What a horrible way to die."

"Can you imagine being buried alive a mile or two under the ground, lying injured in total darkness, wondering if you'd ever be found in time, and all the while listening for the slightest creak that might signal another explosion or cave-in? I hadn't given it much thought until I did this play, and I can tell you, the whole idea of it just freaks me out."

"I couldn't imagine working in the dark all the time. They wouldn't have seen much sun at all, I suppose." I held the cup between my hands as I gazed out the window to the beautiful garden where the colourful flowers were bathing in the sun.

"Especially during the winter when the days are short. They'd go down before dawn and up after dark," said

Gerald as he reached over and took a biscuit and then sat back in his armchair and sipped his tea. We were quiet for a moment as we mulled over the images of the poor miners. As he placed his cup back on the tray, he asked, "Have you heard any Welsh men's choirs?"

"Yes, I was listening to a record recently. It was haunting and mournful but so beautiful. It brought tears to my eyes."

"The men used to sing those songs to keep their spirits up as they headed down the mines, because they were never sure whether they would surface that day. And then as they came out of the mines they'd sing again, this time with relief."

"Maybe that's the feeling I identified in the music. Lamentation. You said the mines have improved now?"

"Absolutely, but it's because of people like Keir Hardy. He used his parliamentary position to expose the companies that exploited the miners, and legislated for compensation and enforced safety measures."

"I guess a lot of people didn't like what he was trying to do," I said.

"No, especially because it hurt their hip pocket. He received a lot of opposition, but in the end he got the changes he was lobbying for. Anyway, here's the script. Read it through. It will help you to understand more about it."

So I joined the theatre group as they travelled around the United Kingdom performing about four times a week. I played the role of a pollster, which was a clever scripting device to include a commentator. My opening lines included the word "today". To the British ear, my Aussie accent made this sound like "to die", which confused the audience. I ended up at the end of the tour sounding very English as I worked at rounding my vowels.

In each venue the cast was billeted in private homes. For one of the performances we travelled to a rather small village in Wales, where we were to perform the play in the shadow of a coal mine that over the years had caused thousands of deaths. The atmosphere at the performance that night was imbibed with painful memories, as most of the audience was related to miners both past and present. Knowing this, the cast's emotions were heightened and the performance was powerful. There were real tears, instead of acted crying. More pauses were noticeable as the actors struggled to control their cracking voices. We felt one with these people and through the play we were telling them that we understood their pain and anger.

But something else happened the morning of this performance that enabled me to take a big step on my spiritual search. The previous day as we'd travelled towards the village in Wales, some words kept running around in my head. Maybe I had memorised them at some time, but if I had, I could only remember some of the words. I strained my brain to recall the rest of the quote so that I could make sense of it. The harder I tried to bring it to mind, the more it eluded me. "... *and He will make straight your paths.*" The words kept reverberating around my mind as I tried to recapture the rest of this line. I thought it sounded biblical, but I wasn't sure.

That night I was invited to stay with a middle-aged woman. Her neat house was built in a line of identical houses down the street. There were no front gardens, so their front doors, all painted in bright colours, opened straight onto the footpath. She was a very warm person and did everything she could to make me feel welcome. During supper she told me she was a nurse and from the books on the shelf I could tell she was obviously religious. On the lounge room wall was a painting of man, who I assumed was Jesus, knocking on a door. But I noticed the door didn't have a handle. As I learnt later, the artist had not forgotten to paint it in. The omission was significant.

"I'm so sorry, dear, but unfortunately they have rostered me on the early shift tomorrow. I'll be leaving about 5.30 in the morning. Please just make yourself at home and I'll see you at the play. Is there anything you need?"

"I wondered if you had a Bible I could borrow?"

With great delight she took one off the shelf and handed it to me.

I was anxious to find the rest of the verse that had pestered me all day. So I retired to my room and flipped through the pages, but soon realised it was going to be an impossible task. With embarrassment I whispered a little request to God to help me and sat with a pen in my hand thinking that He might plop the verse into my head. I sat for a while and then began to feel very foolish. What a dill I was to think that God would be the least bit interested in such a stupid little thing. I gave up and went to bed.

Next morning I went into the kitchen. My host had laid the table and written a note with instructions for breakfast. While reading the note, I noticed there was a Bible coordinate printed in red lettering at the top of the page, next to a small picture of a flower. All it said was "Proverbs 3:5, 6".

It was obviously a Christian notepad. I finished reading her note and went to throw it in the bin. Then something checked me. I fetched the Bible, and held my breath as I fumbled through to the book of Proverbs.

"Trust in the Lord with all your heart, and do not rely on your

own understanding. In all your ways acknowledge Him, and He will make straight your paths."

A smile etched itself across my face as I eased into the chair. Another ray of light had permeated my soul. The God whom I was searching for was also reaching out to me in a very personal way, showing me that He was very interested in the small details of my life.

I clung to that verse in the Bible because what was about to eventuate over the next 12 months was certainly beyond my own understanding.

Beyond the veil

It was a few days before Christmas, and I was back at Tirley Garth in Chester. Gherkin was back in Germany for the holidays and I was in bed with a bad cold. A few days earlier Anne had spent a couple of nights with me on her way back from Sweden. Her year-long leave was up and to keep her teaching position she needed to be back at work in Australia by the beginning of the school year at the end of January.

In so many ways I longed to go with her, as I was homesick. I was not looking forward to spending Christmas in the cold of England instead of being in the warm summer at home with my family. I waved goodbye to Anne as the train pulled out from the little village station, en route to London and the airport. I stood alone on the platform watching the train as it clacked along the track until it went around a bend. Although I enjoyed the sense of individuality when I was away from Anne, I missed our natural affinity and friendship. The thought of her going so far away from me again made me really sad and I felt bereft. Tears streamed down my face as I walked slowly out of the station. The night before I had explained why I could not go back with her.

"Anne, I really want to go home with you tomorrow, but

I seem to be on this important journey of discovery which I sense has more to offer."

"What about your job at the Guide Dog Centre? What's happening with that?" Anne placed her case on the bed and proceeded to pull everything out.

When my three months' leave was up I had felt like I'd just scratched the surface of what I was searching for. I couldn't expect them to keep my position any longer, so I'd resigned. It was a really hard thing to do, because I really loved the work.

"Well, you know I had to resign. I'm hoping there may still be a position for me when I get home, but I'm not sure."

Anne was leaning over the bed, repacking her case. She straightened up and turned to face me. "So, how long do you expect to be here for? When we spoke in July at the IOC conference in Switzerland you thought you might be heading home by now."

I sat next to her case on the bed looking down at the floor. "Actually, I'm not too sure when I'll be home. I think this is an amazing interlude in life that offers me a chance to work some things out. I mean, it's not always easy living in this community. You know some of the ideas of IOC can be challenging. And I'm having disturbed sleeps with all these night-time interferences."

"Oh stop there. That absolutely freaks me out. I really don't want to hear about it!" She leant over again to put the last few things in her case.

"Mmm. Well, I'm glad it's happening to me and not you then. So I'm just going to stay in the UK until I find some answers."

Anne shut her suitcase and put it on the floor near the

door. She flopped on the bed beside me and put her arm around my shoulders.

"I hope it doesn't take too much longer. I miss you."

Answers come when you least expect them. As I lay in bed feeling miserable with a cold and homesickness there was a knock on the door and in poked the head of my new friend Nessie. She was a secondary school teacher from Cardiff in Wales and had come for part of the Christmas break to visit her father, who was living at Tirley Garth. She was staying in a room near her father in the main building, which was across the big garden from where I was staying.

"Hi, Nessie. It's lovely to see you, but please stay away. I'd hate anyone to catch this rotten cold."

At this, she came in, shut the door and sat at the end of my bed.

"I'd rather catch the cold than know you're lying here all alone and sick at this time of year."

Such a selfless gesture acted on my heart like heat on ice. Tears melted from my previously staunch eyes, as I poured out the story of my sleepless nights. In between the tears and coughing that the cold had brought on, she obviously deciphered the gist of the story.

"It started with footsteps ... then I've felt taps on the shoulder ... and sometimes gasping under the pillow. That really freaks me out because it's so close to me, and I just nearly die each time. It's right in my ear. Oh and then there's the fingernails scraping down the cupboard. It's really eerie. Nobody else can hear it though. But I'm not imagining it, really, I'm not, I'm really quite sane ... although I am very tired. I think it's an evil spirit. I've already had a run-in with one of those. Oh God, what will I do, Nessie?"

I opened my hanky and buried my face, sobbing. I had

revealed it all but I didn't care. I felt the tension drain out through the tears.

Nessie had listened with such empathy, nodding like she understood. She slid up the bed and wrapped her arms around me in a comforting hug.

"There is someone who I know can help you," said Nessie as she sat back in her spot at the end of the bed, tucking her feet under the blanket. "He's a friend of mine called Dr Kenneth McCall. He likes to be known as Ken."

"You really think he knows about all this sort of stuff?" I asked hopefully while mopping the tears from my face. I plumped up a pillow behind me and leant back while Nessie told me some background about Dr McCall.

He had been a Congregational missionary in Northern China during the years of the Sino-Japanese War. At that time he was a surgeon. One evening he was tramping along a dirt road, delivering some medical supplies to a hospital in an outlying settlement. Suddenly a man dressed all in white came up behind him and pointed to a village at right angles to where he was headed, telling him that there were wounded people there who needed his help. The man and Ken headed off in the new direction. They arrived at the village gates, and the villagers opened them and pulled the doctor inside. The man in white was nowhere to be seen. The villagers told Ken that he had narrowly avoided a Japanese ambush and the hospital where he had been heading was now overrun.

"So who was this man in white who had warned him?" I asked Nessie.

"Well, this is the thing. He asked around about a man dressed in white and nobody had ever seen him. On reflection, Ken recalled that the man had spoken to him in

English, and as he knew all the foreigners in the area, of which this man was not one, Ken came to believe that the man was Jesus."

"Wow. That's amazing. So was it?"

"Who really knows? I believe it though or maybe an angel because up to this point Ken had not yet discovered his life's work which has helped thousands of people. He was not meant to die that day."

"What is his work?" I asked through a cough.

"I'm getting to that, but I think it will help if I tell you how he became interested in this particular work," said Nessie, as she moved to the armchair next to the heater. "Soon after this incident, Ken and his wife were interned in a Japanese prisoner of war camp for four years, and when they were finally released and returned to Britain he decided to study psychology. During his years in China he had observed some inexplicable things that he couldn't brush aside. He was particularly troubled by the memory of a 'devil mad' or *keng kuei* man who had been cured of his madness by the intervention of an ordinary woman with a prayer. This man was berserk. In the West his breakdown would have been attributed to the intolerable pressures of modern society. But in that remote village on the northern plains of China the people just knew that something evil had taken possession of him and that it needed to be cast out.

"The villagers at first called on their witch doctor's white magic and tried the herbalist's sedatives. When this failed they chained the victim to a wall to be stoned to death. It might sound barbaric, but the people thought that the evil had to go from the man by any means. After they stoned him, he didn't die quickly. The people interpreted this as an indication that he could be cured, but that he needed a special sort of help. They didn't call on the mission priest or the doctor, but asked one of the many untrained Bible women who devoted their lives to spreading practical Christianity, who nevertheless believed in the Chinese superstitions of good and evil spirits. The little lady went up to the battered bleeding man and began to pray a simple prayer of exorcism, after which the man slumped in his chains unconscious. The villagers took this as a sign of his release from 'devil madness', which it was. He was cured and was able to take his place among them again."

I had been listening intently, wondering why most other cultures believed in evil spirits, but my own discounted it all as superstitious ignorance.

"That's incredible. So do you think this presence I'm experiencing is an evil spirit?"

"No, I don't, actually. It doesn't sound evil. There are two sorts of spirits. Some seem to be evil, often coming as a result of occult practices, while others seem to be neutral and harmless, begging for help. I think in this case it sounds like the latter."

"So do you think I need an exorcism? I saw that movie a few years ago and it scared the heck out of me."

Nessie laughed encouragingly. "No, no. You're not possessed. Just to finish off Ken's story, he spent years investigating psychiatric diseases, and whether the accepted methods of treatment were the best ways to help the sufferers. He even lived in mental hospitals learning all he could, convinced that there must be a way to reach these people and steer them out of their private mazes."

"And he found a way?"

"He did. Look, I'm so sorry, but I have to pop in to Dad's room and see him before it gets too late. But I'll come and visit you tomorrow and tell you the rest. I just want to assure you that I know he can help you."

"So he's still alive then?"

"Very much so. He is about 75 but is still very active. He lives in England down south, in the New Forest. Don't you worry. I knew I was meant to come and see you today. Now I know why."

With that she gave me another big reassuring hug and left. I snuggled up under the blankets feeling their warmth and also the warmth deep inside that I had felt in Wales when I'd been given the Bible passage, and also when the little woodpecker had lived. I knew the answer was coming. My whole view of the world and my personal belief system were about to undergo a dramatic recantation.

Healing the family tree
(Julie with Ken & Francis McCall)

Healing the family tree

The next day I was feeling much better. The garden was covered with a dusting of snow, and fog was hovering just above the ground. It was the first time I was to experience a white Christmas. Back home we would be trying to keep ourselves cool. Limp pine trees plunged daily into buckets of water would hopefully stay alive in the heat until Christmas Day. Many families tried to maintain some European traditions of hot roast dinners, mince pies and plum pudding, but gradually people were switching to salads, barbequed prawns, fish and champagne at the beach. Even the pine Christmas trees were being replaced with a branch from a gum tree. I was going to phone home on Christmas Eve, which meant I would reach my family when they were eating Christmas lunch. We were one of the families that stuck to tradition, even down to the brandy butter, custard, cream *and* ice-cream to put on the plum pudding. I felt another pang of homesickness and decided a walk might help.

Donning all the gear to keep warm, including a woollen scarf that I wrapped around my face to keep the icy air from entering my coughing lungs, I wandered through the foggy garden. I could appreciate its charm, but I missed the bright sunlight of home and wondered how long until all the fog disappeared from my life and I could see enough to return home.

When I got back to the house, I made a big pot of tea, covered it with a woollen tea-cosy to keep it warm and collected some mince pies and shortbread which I arranged on a plate decorated with Christmas trees and holly. I placed it all on a large wooden tray, took it back to my room and sat by the window, waiting for Nessie to arrive. My mood had become as dreary as the view out my window while I grappled with the new dimension of life that I needed to explore. On the one hand I embraced it as the possible way out of the haunting and yet I recoiled from it, frightened and threatened by this unseen world that was obviously very powerful.

When Nessie arrived I poured the tea and we munched on the shortbread chatting about ordinary things. After a while I was ready to plunge back into the story.

"So you don't think this thing waking me up is an evil spirit?"

"No, I think it's probably a relative who wants your help."

"A dead relative … needing help … a ghost hanging around? But I've always been told that when you die you go to Heaven or if you're really bad, like a Hitler or someone, you go to Hell and that there is no such things as ghosts."

I felt an emotion like panic rising in me as Nessie attempted to explain.

"Yes, I was brought up believing that too but I think differently now. Ken has been so successful in treating mentally ill patients that I know he's on to something."

"So, am I mentally ill?" I whispered not sure that I wanted to hear the answer.

"Absolutely not," she said soothingly. "I was going to say that he helps many other people who experience hauntings and other things. He's becoming very well known and sought after. Of course he has had his share of scoffers, but when you consider his record you can't ignore it. Like when he was working in a mental hospital where chronically ill people had been living for up to 40 years. Every treatment had been tried and failed. Ken cured many of them."

"That's pretty convincing. So how did he do it?"

I sensed we were getting close to the answer. Nessie finished her tea, brushed the shortbread crumbs off her lap and tucked her feet up under her.

"What he has realised is that we all make mistakes while we are alive but some things we do seem to prevent us from moving on."

"Really? Like what?"

"There are a number of things. Usually Ken gets you to draw up a family tree. You identify anyone in your family who had a mental illness, had committed suicide, was killed in a war and did not have a funeral, any miscarriages or abortions, any hereditary diseases and so on. And then there are the areas that cause lots of problems, like being involved with witchcraft or the occult. Actually he has written a book called *Healing the family tree*. He has mentioned more of the things in there."

As Nessie was talking, I was taking a mental note of our family. We had quite a number of these things. I asked Nessie where the dead people were if they had not moved on.

"Many of the people Ken had worked with would say things like, "There is no day and no night in my world." The dead who have not been released into the eternal world, are still earthbound. They are lost and looking for rest. Ken calls this place *no man's land*.

"These discarnate spirits manifest themselves by interfering with the living, either malevolently or by seeking help. They want to appeal to those who are sensitive, prayerful and sympathetic, preferably a descendant or a trusted family member. If they can't find such a person, they will haunt the places where they died since they can no longer help themselves. In life they failed to deal with their mistakes, either because they didn't have the opportunity to make the decisions in life, or ignored the ultimate issues. At death, neither they nor the living were able to put right their unfinished business."

This explanation sounded feasible, even though it contradicted everything I'd ever thought about the dead.

"How do you help them, I mean, how can I help whoever this is? And why do you think it came to me? I mean, all my family has been to England, even my twin sister. They never had anything like this happen."

"Are you more sensitive than your sister?"

"All the family says I'm oversensitive, that I need to toughen up. I wish I could but I don't know how to."

"Well, I'm sure whoever wants you to help them is glad you didn't. The other thing Ken emphasises is the importance of funerals. The main purpose for the attendance of relatives and friends at funerals is to adequately and honestly present the person to God."

"Is that so? I thought the funeral was more for the living than for the dead. Why can't the departed attend to their issues once they realise?"

"We only have free will in life. Once we die, we no longer have that opportunity."

"So what you are saying is that the living can do it for them."

This was getting close. I took some deep breaths to steady the rising excitement, and also nervousness as I waited to hear what I could do.

"Yes, exactly. We need to apologise to God, on behalf of them, and commit each one back to Him."

"Is that all? It sounds too simple."

"It is and it isn't. You can't just rattle off all the names. It has to be well thought out – reflectively, thoughtfully and with heartfelt emotion. Also, you need to address anything in your own life that is not right."

"Oh, that could take a while," I said, mischievously needing to lighten the conversation for a moment.

Nessie laughed and straightened her legs out. I poured us another cup of tea, and heaped two spoonfuls of sugar into mine. We sipped the tea in silence, and ate the mince pies.

Nessie was looking kindly at me with her clear blue eyes, realising I needed to digest all that she'd said. So many things were darting in and out of my mind. For the first time I dared to confront the possibility that the choices we make while alive not only have an impact on the direction of our lives, but also on our deaths. I wondered if this was the same as the law of karma that Hindus believe in. But she had not mentioned that if we get it wrong in this life we would come back as an inferior animal or a less evolved soul. No, it was like the spirits still want to find eternal peace, but get stuck and need help from the living to show them the way.

"Do you think I should have a go at drawing up my family tree?"

"Yes, why not. Then we can call Ken, and he can direct

you. Sometimes he can pick immediately who is pestering you from what you show on your tree."

"Really?"

"Oh, yes. And sometimes he actually sees the person as well. He's so nonplussed by it all, treats it as quite normal. He suggests a person should spend a few days working on it. You need to have space around you and do it thoughtfully. It can take a while for things to come to mind."

"OK, but how far back do you need to go? I mean what if I don't know it all?"

"None of us know it all, but Ken can see patterns in family trees that tell him what the problem might be. Also you will know enough to do what the spirit wants you to do for them. You might have only heard a story once, but it will now come to mind to give the clue as to what is needed."

"Gosh, it's all so … so supernatural, like a scary movie or something. It's not that I don't believe it, I think I do, but it's so outside anything I've ever been taught or wanted to know about. One thing is worrying me though. From Sunday school classes, years ago, I remember we had a talk after reading something from the Bible. I'm sure it said that we are forbidden to contact the dead. It's got a name, a funny word … 'acra' something."

"Acromancy. Yes, it is totally forbidden, but you are not contacting them or talking to them. They have come to you, asking for help and you don't talk to them. You pray for them. There is a big difference."

It was all making sense on one level, but I was finding it so difficult to move into this way of thinking. And yet logic and need demanded that I consider it. I felt completely drained. It was like part of me wanted to go to sleep and forget all about what I had heard.

"Yes, I see. There is a difference, isn't there. Maybe I'll have a go at the family tree then. I guess it wouldn't hurt, would it?"

"It can't do any harm, and might do a lot of good, right?"

"Absolutely. Actually, I'm suddenly feeling really tired. I might have to deal with it later. Is that alright?"

"Of course. I know it's all very confronting. You'll need some time to get your head around it all. Dad's asked me to drive him down to London today so he can visit an old family friend. We'll stay overnight. I'll come and see you when we get back."

I walked her to the front door and gave her a big hug. She looked at me with an encouraging "it's going to be alright" look, and walked towards her old burgundy Mini Minor. After a couple of tries it spluttered and started. She wound the car window right down so she could put her whole arm out to give me an enthusiastic wave and then drove off down the slippery driveway towards her father's residence on the other side of the huge property.

I didn't feel like going back to the room. I fought the tiredness and realised I was churned up and finding it hard to think, like the fog had seeped into my brain. If I really accepted all Nessie had said, then I was challenged in every area of my life. It demanded an enormous leap into areas that I wanted to avoid. I bundled up in my coat, hat, scarf and gloves once again, and went out into the garden. The weak winter sun had only managed to burn off some of the fog, but it was much clearer than it had been earlier. Nobody else seemed to be out, which was a relief because I didn't want to be distracted from the internal debate that was reverberating around every cell of my brain, demanding a decision. I spoke out loud to the trees, the squirrels and to

God if He was listening. I hoped He was. I took the side of my initial beliefs, and then the side of the new challenging belief, debating with myself as I walked around and around the vast property. After a long while I headed towards the garden seat overlooking a pond. I sat down, staring into the water, dazed from the internal struggle. Presently the water that had appeared muddy looking and dull began to sparkle and become clear so that I could see an orange fish swimming around. I looked up to see the sun had finally burned through the fog and was smiling briefly on the winter's day.

It was then that I made the decision to move forward on this part of my spiritual journey which at this stage was very foreign and scary.

The next morning was clear and crisp. More snow had fallen during the night and was lying on the branches of the spruce trees, turning the garden seat white while the fence posts around the house wore little snow hats. There were an animal's footprints imprinted in the fresh snow where it had walked across the lawn heading towards the bird feeder, which was kept supplied with wild bird seed throughout the year. It probably liked to eat the spilt seed underneath the feeder.

I pulled the little table and chair beneath the window so I could look out, and sat down with pen and paper. This was the moment to begin. I had been pondering it since the day before and had whispered a prayer for help. I started drawing up our family tree beginning with my generation. Using a red pen, I circled the individuals according to the guidelines Dr McCall had suggested. There was a cousin who had committed suicide and at least one abortion that I knew of. When that was completed, I went back a generation to my parents' time. More there to mark in red. My grandparents' generation slowed me down. I knew more about my maternal than my paternal side. I'd see if my older brother could fill in some gaps as he was interested in family history. I wouldn't need to tell him why, just that I was drawing up our family tree. I checked the time. Yes, I could call him now. It would only be about 9.30 at night.

After we had spoken, I was able to go back as far as our great-grandparents' day. It was ironic that a maternal great-aunt had been part of the Nazi Party in Germany, and had killed herself at the end of the war. On my paternal side there was Jewish blood.

I spent the rest of the day in between meals and walks concentrating on doing this task as thoroughly as I could. During one of the walks, I remembered a story that I had heard as a young girl from my grandmother. I think she had only mentioned it once, and I couldn't recall ever having thought about it again until now. Nan had told me about her mother's sister, Tilly. This would make her my great-great-aunt. Apparently in about 1910, Aunt Tilly had come over to Australia to visit. Not long after her return to England she committed suicide. That was all I knew. A strange little cameo of family history, but I found myself writing her name in bold print and encircling it with a number of red circles.

That evening, when Nessie came over after spending the day with her father, I showed her what I'd done with the family tree. She looked at it carefully.

"This is really quite thorough. Well done. There is certainly a lot here to address."

She glanced up to notice me turning away with embarrassment.

"Oh, don't you worry. All families have things that should be dealt with in this way, some more than others. I've seen many trees much worse than yours. It's just good that you're prepared to do something about it."

That placated me.

"Why have you marked this one specifically ... what's her name ... Tilly?"

"I don't know really. I was told about her by my grandmother when I was a little girl and out of the blue the story came into my head."

"Mmm, that's significant. Why don't we phone Ken? I've already told him that you would probably call, and he might be able to help you over the phone."

As it was Christmas Eve, I was hesitant to disturb him, but Nessie assured me he wouldn't mind. After a short chat with him, Nessie handed me the phone. He listened as I told him what I had been experiencing at night over the past six months, interrupting me when he needed further clarification. His voice was cultured and calm, as he talked about the departed. As he mentioned them, his voice cracked and I could detect he was weeping quietly. Nessie explained later that he often did that as he felt so deeply for these lost spirits.

At his request I ran through the generations on my tree with him. I could tell he was taking notes. When I'd finished he was quiet for a while.

"We have a number of people here that need prayer, certainly. Can you tell me any more about this suicide, Tilly?"

I glanced up at Nessie who was waiting patiently and she understood that he had said something significant. He hadn't seen my drawing of the family tree with the extra red marks on this name and yet he had picked her out.

"I don't know much, only that she returned to England and killed herself."

"She suffocated in some way."

"Dr McCall, how can you possibly know that?"

"Because of the gasping under your pillow and the scratching noises on the wardrobe, I believe she died by suffocation."

"Oh," was all I could manage. He believed this was the person who was bothering me. Yet she wasn't trying to scare me, just get my attention. She needed my help. I was also determined to ask my grandmother how she had died.

"Um, Dr McCall, if this is true, then what should I do?"

"You need to offer her up to God and apologise on her behalf for taking her own life. The best place to do this, if you are in the Christian tradition, is at a Eucharist service in a church."

This was beginning to sound very religious. A number of years ago I had decided that church was irrelevant and if there was a God, there had to be more to it than listening to a boring clergyman in a cold church once a week.

"I don't go to church, Dr McCall."

"Please call me Ken. Well, I suggest you do. I have found with suicides, offering them up sincerely and with love at a Eucharist five times usually frees them to continue their journey to Heaven."

"Five times. Alright, that sounds fair enough. I can do that."

I thought that sounded quite easy to do and I could put up with going to church for a while if it meant I was free of Aunt Tilly.

I found a really ancient Church of England near Tirley Garth, so I began to go there and pray for my great-great-aunt Tilly, especially during the Eucharist service. I had been doing that for four consecutive Sundays and the following Sunday was Easter Sunday. This would be the fifth time I had offered Aunt Tilly up in prayer at the Eucharist in a church, which was significant, according to what Ken had told me. Nessie realised it also and thought it would be special to do that service in the beautiful Anglican Cathedral near where she lived in Cardiff, Wales. So she invited me to travel to Cardiff to stay with her.

We decided I would drive her dad back so they could spend Easter together. Nessie was staying in the family home, but since her mother had died many years earlier and her father was residing at Tirley Garth in Chester, Nessie lived there on her own. So she was looking forward to filling up some of the empty bedrooms for a few days.

Easter Sunday arrived, and we were able to walk to the cathedral. With as much belief as I could muster, and it really hadn't been that much, I asked God to forgive my auntie and to accept her in His heavenly realm.

As Nessie and I walked out of the church into the sunny spring morning, I said with relief, "Well, good riddance, Aunt Tilly. Now maybe I can get some sleep."

Nessie hooked her arm through mine and whispered in my ear, "I don't think you should say that."

"Why not? Ken said it would take five Eucharists and I've done that. It's behind me. Now I want to forget all this and get on with living and the living."

Nessie smiled at me and said nothing more.

That night I went to my room prepared for an uninterrupted night. As I was hanging up my clothes I thought I heard someone in the room. I looked around and smiled to myself. The last six months had affected my nerves. Everything was fine now. I had been to five communion services; she was free and could leave me alone.

With a big sigh of relief I flopped into bed and turned off the light. As soon as I was still I could clearly hear someone in my room whizzing around as if very agitated. Although I couldn't see, I followed the noise around the room. Who was this? Was it still Aunt Tilly refusing to leave or was it someone else? I froze in the bed, listening and watching, wondering what to do.

Then I felt my bed being shaken.

That did it. Catapulting off the bed I charged into Nessie's room shaking violently and almost screaming, "It didn't work. Nessie, it didn't work. I'm never going to be free of this, it's followed me and it's in this room, listen … over there … now there near the chair, hear it?" I swivelled around pointing in the direction of the presence.

"No, I can't hear anything, but I can sense something. OK, push the other bed over this way. Sleep in here. Tomorrow we'll call Ken."

We pushed the single beds together and I ended up holding her hand all night. I could hear Aunt Tilly, or whoever, walking around the room and at times tapping me on the shoulder. My head was overwrought with the thought of dead relatives, and God and punishment and no man's land and evil and curses. That night everything morphed through me until I thought that maybe I *was* going mad.

Morning finally came. I was still agitated as I called Ken to tell him what had happened. Again the calm, undaunted voice began to settle me.

"She is obviously a very timid spirit and probably needs a communion service just for her. I suggest you come and stay at my home in the New Forest and we will arrange a minister to hold the service. Let's see ... What about the week after next. You can travel down on Sunday and we can plan the service for Tuesday. Does that suit?"

"Oh, yes, absolutely. Thank you so much, Ken."

Nessie and I arranged to head down to spend a few days with Ken and his wife. In the meantime, I called my grandmother and asked her as nonchalantly as I could how Great-Great-Aunt Tilly had died. I was wondering if she had really suffocated. The answer she gave convinced me that we were on the right track.

"She threw herself in the Thames and drowned," replied Grandmother.

Driving down to the New Forest I was determined to be brave. I taught Nessie a traditional Australian children's song ... "Kookaburra sits in the old gum tree" which we did in a round. We stopped off for lunch at an old country pub and sat for a while in the sunny courtyard enjoying a glass of wine.

We pulled up at Dr McCall's house just on dusk. It was an old rambling house set within a stretch of forest and had once been the home of Conan Doyle, the writer of the Sherlock Holmes stories. A stream ran along the border of the forest, marking the boundary of his land. Ken and his wife had raised five children here and now regularly welcomed numerous grandchildren. We parked the car and walked over a wooden bridge under which ran a tiny tributary of the border stream. On the left side of the path facing anybody who was coming to visit was a small cannon, obviously a collector's item but Nessie and I exchanged a look that said, "An odd thing to have at your entrance."

Before this thought took hold, down the path with a broad smile came Mrs McCall, herself a doctor. She was very friendly and embraced us warmly, inviting us to come into the kitchen where she had prepared supper.

"Call me Francis," she said as she turned to lead us into the house. As we were entering, I noticed carved gargoyles on the corners of the roof.

The room was a country kitchen with rustic wooden furniture. Two of the walls were lined with cabinets displaying blue-patterned crockery. The big pots on the stove emitted delicious smells which made me realise how hungry I was. As Francis prepared the gravy she chatted away making us feel at ease and welcome in her home. It was obvious to me that she was a very practical, no nonsense sort of woman who had successfully raised five children, while continuing in her profession as a family doctor. I wondered what she thought about her husband's "work" and theories.

She was about to serve up dinner when in walked Ken. He greeted Nessie with a hug, and then shook my hand. He wore a pale shirt, coloured knitted tie and a brown woollen cardigan with leather patches on the elbows. He was not very tall and his head was balding, but his dark brown eyes really looked at me from behind his glasses and were kind.

"Let's sit down, it smells delicious, Francis," he said and then bowed his head to say grace.

Over dinner he talked about his friends in Australia. After a while Nessie asked him about some of the people he had helped. As he talked about the restless souls, his voice quivered and tears sprang to his eyes. At first I felt embarrassed, but after a while I accepted that this was his great compassion spilling over and it seemed right. I kept stealing looks at Francis for any signs of disbelief, but I saw none.

He talked about this spirit world as though it was as normal and as obvious to him as the people sitting around the table. By the end of dinner, it seemed less fantastic to me also.

We helped with the dishes. He washed and I was surprised when he didn't use any detergent.

"We don't need all these chemicals. Hot water is all we need. Our bodies and the environment are better off if we limit all these toxins."

This was 1978, and as yet the world's consciousness was not very sensitised to green issues. That came later, so at the time I concluded that he must be a bit eccentric. Francis showed us to our room, which was a big bedroom with three single beds.

"This was the girls' room," she said as she handed us towels. "Breakfast is at seven. Just come down when you're ready. Sleep well."

Nessie and I got into our beds and turned off the light. It was a very dark night and I was feeling very uneasy after hearing all the stories of unsettled spirits and I really hoped Aunt Tilly would leave me alone. I shut my eyes tightly wanting to fall quickly asleep and enter a nice dream world of tropical beaches with clear blue water and wide white sand dunes far away from the New Forest and spirits and cannons and gargoyles.

After a while Nessie said very quietly, "JF," – this was the nickname she had given me – "can you see the light appearing and disappearing on the wall?"

I turned over opened my eyes and waited for them to focus.

"Oh my gosh, I can. What is it? Not anything else, surely. I'm not sure I can take any more!"

We both watched in silence as periodically a light appeared on the wall and then disappeared.

"I think it's Christ," said Nessie with an ethereal whisper.

We stayed there glued to our beds for about half an hour as memories of the night's discussions whirled round our heads.

"Please, Nessie, could you turn the light on?" I was feeling weak with fear.

She bravely got out of bed but headed to the window instead of the door where the light switch was. Peering out the window, she paused for a while and then started to laugh. I certainly did not feel like laughing.

"What on earth is wrong with you? This is just too scary. I wish we had stayed in a nice little B&B." At that I pulled the doona over my head.

"Oh, JF, it's the headlights from the cars out on the road. The road is quite a way from here, but as they take the bend the lights flash in here." She fell back on her bed laughing a bit too loudly. I realised she was very relieved, but also disappointed that it was not Christ paying us a visit.

The next morning Ken had arranged for an Anglican minister whom he often worked with to come and hold the service for Aunt Tilly. I had made a copy of the rest of the family tree to be placed on the altar.

The minister looked as if he was in his mid-forties and was dressed in a black hassock with a Bible and another book tucked under his arm. His faded blond hair fell over his forehead as he bowed his head in prayer. His voice was authoritative and he began the service by asking the angels to bring anyone from my family who was meant to be at this Eucharist. I imagined Great-Great-Aunt Tilly standing next to the minister in a long dusky pink dress listening to him. It was a bit like a funeral service but with special Bible readings talking about God's love and forgiveness. We then participated in communion, receiving the bread and wine.

After the formal service was over, the paper on which I had written the names of my family was ceremoniously burned. This was to signify that all had been taken care of. I wondered if Aunt Tilly had really gone this time and whether she had turned to me with a wave and a smile, grateful that I had helped her.

"Goodbye, Aunt Tilly. I hope you have found peace," I whispered as I glanced upwards. I did not see anything, but as I looked at Ken, he was looking to his left towards a blank wall, smiling and nodding at someone. That night I slept better than I had for nearly a year. Aunt Tilly did not visit me again.

We stayed with Ken for the rest of the week as we met a number of families he was working with, learning more about his extraordinary work. One of the cases that I found particularly confronting, as it challenged existing societal ideas and therefore also my ideas, was related to when life begins.

Ken had taken us to a country church where a special service was being held for a young man called Alistair. At 12 years old he had begun to suffer from what was labelled "epilepsy". He was now 22 and after years of various medications being tried with little effect, the family decided to seek Ken's help. As we drove to the church, Ken told us that the service was being held for Alistair's sibling who had been aborted 30 years ago. I struggled to see any connection between an aborted baby and a 22-year-old man having "fits", but Ken continued talking as if what he had just said was not at all unusual.

"I have worked with over 600 families who came to me with children suffering from mental and physical problems. By tracing their family trees we found a number of babies who had been aborted, miscarried, stillborn or discarded at birth. They had never been loved by being named and recognised by their parents nor had they been properly committed to God in a burial service. What I have learnt and observed is that these human souls try to get attention from their family members."

My great-grandfather's desire to give his child a funeral service even though it left him broke came to my mind, but this memory was usurped by a momentous question that I needed to ask. I was thinking about a friend of mine who had become pregnant in her first year of university and whom I had encouraged to "get rid of it" before it developed into a "proper" baby.

"But when does a tiny embryo become a real person? I thought it was just a group of cells until … well, I don't know quite when. That's what the doctors say, just a group of cells no bigger than a grain of rice."

My voice sounded loud in the car as the alarm at what I was realising tightened my throat.

Ken glanced at me in the rear-view mirror before he explained. His voice began to quiver like it did when he talked about the departed.

"Maybe so, but at six weeks old these 'cells' have a heart with two chambers, which has started beating. There is a head with simple eyes and ears. The beginnings of arms, legs and backbone can be distinctly seen."

He wiped away the tears that rolled down his face as I sat in stunned silence tightly gripping Nessie's hand while my reason and emotions did battle.

Ken glanced at me again in the rear-view mirror and obviously saw my puzzled distress. After a few moments' silence he switched from doctor to theologian.

"There are a number of places in the Bible that suggest when life starts. For example, in Jeremiah 1:5 God says, *'Before you were conceived in your mother's womb I knew you.'* [1]

"There are many other statements like this," continued Ken, "so we can conclude that at the moment of conception there exists a real being, a soul, a temporary resident residing within the body. Other cultures believe this too. In Japan, for example, the Buddhists have a ceremony called the *Mizuko Kuyo* ritual or 'water baby ceremony' which is a 'fetus memorial service' for the unborn dead, which has happened either through miscarriage, abortion or being stillborn. Originally it was performed to placate the potential retribution of a vengeful spirit. Today it is also a way for mothers to outwardly mourn their dead child. It's yet another proof to me that mothers just *know* there is more to what is growing inside them than a mere group of cells."

We pulled up at a typical English country church nestled amidst a garden and an old cemetery. Ken went inside and conversed with the Anglican minister and then greeted Alistair and his mother. A handful of other people were also present so Nessie and I sat up the back. I was feeling unsettled from this radical new thought and wanted to know what was about to happen in this church service.

---

[1] Jeremiah 1:5.

"It's a bit like a funeral service," said Nessie who had more understanding of what Ken had been talking about. "They will have some readings from the Bible, some prayers and a sort of confession from the mother who needs to ask for forgiveness both from her child and from God for what she has done."

Before she could continue, the minister began to speak. I breathed deeply trying to settle the strong emotions threatening to force out a great sad sob that was anchoring my heart. Instead I gasped at the first Bible reading as it seemed to reinforce what Ken had been saying.

"For you formed my inward parts; you knitted me together in my mother's womb. I praise you, for I am fearfully and wonderfully made. Wonderful are your works; my soul knows it very well. My frame was not hidden from you, when I was being made in secret, intricately woven in the depths of the earth. Your eyes saw my unformed substance; in your book were written, every one of them, the days that were formed for me, when as yet there was none of them."[2]

I looked over to Alistair's mother who had her head bowed as the minister continued on with some prayers. Then he paused and waited. It was time for Alistair's mother to verbally acknowledge and apologise for what she had done. She continued to look down without saying anything. Ken left his seat at the side of the church and went over to her and talked softly with her. She shook her head and whispered something. Suddenly Alistair jumped up and with agitation walked around and around pointing to his mother with a weird look on his face. His mother had her head down weeping and did not look up. He was quite lucid, yet he

---

2   Psalm 139:13-16.

was not himself. He kept pacing around in a semicircle; the service continued as if nothing was happening.

After the second reading which was about the disciples trying to stop the children from bothering Jesus,[3] Ken again spoke to Alistair's mother. This time she lifted her head and gently said a name. Immediately Alistair stopped pacing and sat down. His facial expression appeared normal again. After a final prayer the service was over. Although it had only taken about 20 minutes, it seemed much longer.

As we were driving home, Ken told us that this family would need another service at least, as the mother was not convinced that her decision all those years ago could be affecting her son now. She was not truly sorry nor convinced that what she had done had betrayed one of the first commandments that God gave to His people.[4]

"I think she is suffering greatly," Ken explained, "but she finds it too hard to face the truth of it all. She has not been involved with the church for years and thinks the laws that God gave to Moses are not that relevant anymore."

"Is that the Ten Commandments?" I was wondering if he was serious about those ancient laws. But instead of asking him about their relevance I instead made a statement based on my ignorance. "I'm not sure how they have anything to do with all this."

"Well, the Fifth Commandment says: *'You shall not kill.'* When you understand about the beginnings of life in the womb, then to abort it means you are killing a child, even though it is as tiny as a bit of rice." Ken sounded teary again although his voice was determined. "The problem is, Alistair's mother is in denial, but until she accepts it and can

---

3 Luke 18:16.
4 Exodus 20:13.

offer her departed baby the love he is craving and a sincere apology, this case will drag on, I'm afraid."

"You said 'he'. Do you know it's a boy then?"

"Normally in my experience the departed child or person will seek out a family member of their own sex to help them."

"And does helping them help the family?"

"Absolutely. I have worked with hundreds of families who have experienced remarkable healings after this ministry. Being a doctor I just naturally take notes and I've decided to collate some of these case histories and put them into a book.[5] I'm hoping many others will be helped by it."

My mind was whirling as were my emotions while I struggled to mesh this information with my belief system. Where was the loving God that I had been taught about? I thought that if we lived a good enough life, God would whisk us away into Heaven forgiving everything, especially if you were a little baby. All this entanglement between the living and the dead was like something out of a spooky novel. But what if my understanding of the Almighty and His mysterious ways had been limited? What if there was a whole dimension to life and death that as yet I had not discovered?

Nessie reached over and patted my arm, realising my inner struggle. I knew she had spent many a time talking with Ken and had obviously worked through many of the questions I had. But at this stage I could not reconcile all these new ideas. It would take many years and another encounter with a departed soul for the idea to really hit home.

---

[5] *Healing the family tree* by Dr Kenneth McCall, Sheldon Press, 1982.

Within a few months after the time spent with Ken McCall, I felt ready to return home. It had certainly taken longer to find some answers than the initial three months I had asked for at work. It was closer to 18 months and during that time I had resigned from my job, broken off the engagement (which I did not have the courage to do before I left home) and had been turned inside out spiritually.

As my plane approached Melbourne Airport, the sun was beginning to rise and the whole sky glowed red and orange. After we left the plane and I walked through the gates, I saw my mother waiting and looking in my direction, but I was surprised that she was not running towards me.

When I reached her, before I could say anything she said to me, "Excuse me, are you off that Qantas flight?"

"Mum, it's me. It's me, Julie." I was flabbergasted that she had not recognised me.

She tilted her head, searching my face. Then her expression changed and her eyes lit up.

"Oh, it is too. My goodness, you look so different, I didn't recognise you. I honestly didn't recognise you. It's only been a year and a half, but there is something quite different about you. Oh, come here," she said as she lunged forward wrapping me in one of those maternal embraces that says, *we missed you, we love you, welcome home*.

I had changed and it was so thorough that it had affected my physical appearance. The time out of my regular life had served to draw the dissected parts of myself together and to implant deeply into my soul an awareness of God. But the journey to find a place that accepted the experience of my restless spirit auntie would be long, difficult and lonely.

Time to sift and sort

The awakened spirit within me longed for company in which to share the experiences of the past couple of years and to develop friendships with other people who thought about spiritual things. I began by looking for a church to go to. Opening up the telephone book, I looked at the plethora of Christian churches. Thinking that all churches were pretty much the same, I decided to go to a Baptist Church not far from where I lived. Then I contacted a Bible study group. Most of the people in this group came from the Baptist Church or the Church of Christ. This group emphasised the importance of memorising passages of Scripture, *to have the word of God laid upon your heart.*

    I faithfully used their small printed cards with set Bible verses and learnt the selected Scriptures. The other activity that this group propagated was the responsibility of all Christians to "witness" to those poor lost souls who had not given their "hearts to Jesus", and would therefore end up in Hell.

    In the Baptist Church and the Bible study group the same message was given. You had to personally confess that you had sinned and that Jesus is your Lord and Saviour and ask Him to come into your life. If you did that, it was assured, you would go to Heaven … *"If you confess with your mouth that Jesus is Lord and believe in your heart that God raised him from the dead, you will be saved."* [6]

I talked to a couple of the women in the group about my experience with Aunt Tilly. They thought I was imagining it all, or if it had been real, that was not good. It was certainly not based on Scripture, they said, and I should just put it behind me. Well, I knew it had not been wrong or bad because I had discovered the reality of God through it. But I decided to put it behind me and not to talk about it again. As the experience was so precious to me, I found it very difficult to realise that other people dismissed it as fanciful and wrong theologically. But I learnt a number of things when I was in this group and more importantly I met the wonderful man who was to become my husband.

Although on one level Anne was happy for me to be getting married, on another level she found it really hard. She wanted to be taking this step too but as yet had not met the right person. We also recognised that marriage would impact our twinship, but in exactly what way we weren't sure. Interestingly my future husband, Rob, was also a twin, although his twin was a girl. As a "fraternal" twin, Rob and his sister did not look alike but shared some similar experiences with Anne and me.

Robert and I were married in the Uniting Church. At the very moment we were saying our vows, the sun shone brightly through a narrow window seemingly illuminating us. I felt it was another kiss from Heaven. We began attending a very active Baptist Church. The sermons were good, so was the singing, and there were many other activities outside of Sunday to become involved in. I was realising that not all Christian churches taught the same things. Baptism,

---

6   Romans 10:9, 10.

for example, meant different things to the many different church denominations. Although I had been christened in the Methodist Church and Rob in the Presbyterian Church as babies, the Baptist Church did not recognise it. They did not believe in infant baptism/christening because to the Baptists, baptism should be a witness of your personal decision to accept Jesus as your Lord and Saviour, and a baby cannot make that decision. So when I was nine months pregnant with our first child, Rob and I were baptised by full immersion in a small tiled pool in the corner of the Baptist Church. I was preparing to enter into the spirit of it all by imagining I was dying with Christ and then rising with him as I came out of the water. Unfortunately the minister had omitted to tell me that the heating device had broken. The water was absolutely freezing, and all I could think about was that it was going to cause me to go into labour at any second!

A little visitor

Our daughter was born on a cold winter's morning 18 months after our son's birth. From the moment I saw her little face all scrunched up and heard her screaming protests, I knew we would share a special bond. Katie was nearly four months old when I developed a sharp pain in the right-hand side of my stomach. It continued to get worse, until one night an ambulance took me to hospital. The doctor whipped out my appendix. This, however, was not the problem. In the vicinity of the appendix was some "foreign solid matter" which was sent off to pathology for diagnosis. As it was the weekend, it was going to take longer to process. I heard whispers from the staff of a "precancerous growth".

Finally, after a few days, the doctor walked in briskly with my file open. He was a very abrupt man, the sort that would not put up with any nonsense even if he were giving you bad news.

"Well, it has taken a while to work this one out. They were testing for a malignancy, you know."

"I overheard something, but nobody has said anything yet. So have I got cancer?"

I asked the question as if it were about someone else. During the waiting time I had felt nothing or maybe I was numb with fear at the thought of facing the horrible reality.

"No, you haven't. It was a lump of fetal tissue that must have been displaced during the C section when you delivered your daughter."

"Fetal tissue? So did it come from my daughter? Is she missing something?"

I could not quite grasp what he was saying. He glanced at his watch, obviously impatient to finish his rounds and leave.

"No, of course not. You were probably having twins and one didn't survive past the first few weeks. So you'll be fine to leave the day after tomorrow. Come for a check-up in a month."

He walked out.

I was stunned. Another baby, a twin to my little Katie. What had gone wrong? Had I caused it? Was Katie affected in any way? What about its little soul? My mind immediately went back to all I had learnt about in England regarding the beginning of life. "*At the moment of conception,*" Dr McCall had assured me, "*the soul enters the tiny, yet growing human being.*"[7]

As I lay in the hospital bed I thought about the times I had tried to find a theological place for the "restless spirit" experience. I had asked a Baptist preacher. He thought it was heretical thinking. Then I had sought out a Uniting Church minister who told me it was all a trick of the devil. Finally I asked an Anglican minister's wife who told me it was anti-biblical and not to talk about it to anybody. With no hook on which to hang this unusual part of my life, I had consciously put it into the past. As time went by it began to seem unreal, like in a memory enfolded in fog. Anyway, it belonged to a different person. I felt quite detached from

---

7 Jeremiah 1:5.

that single woman who had searched the world for answers to life. The Christian faith within the Baptist Church was where Rob and I thought we belonged, and unlike the "old me" who had time to travel and explore, I now had a new role as a wife and mother. When I took on my husband's name at our marriage, it had somehow completed this new identity.

So sitting up in the hospital bed, without much sentiment, I said a quick prayer for the baby, Katie's twin, and then tried to push it from my mind and concentrate on getting better.

The next few years sped by as I cared for my two young children. Peter was a placid fellow and was always interested in doing something constructive or musical. He played happily with his little sister, as did she with him. But Katie was always asking me for a sister from the time she could talk. A natural question for a little girl I thought. When I became pregnant again, I explained to her that I was having another baby and that it just might be a girl. Some evenings as Rob and I relaxed together, I thought I heard someone walking around long after bedtime. I mentioned it to him but he assumed it was air in the pipes or another house noise, so I refused to believe it could be anything else.

Our bedroom was at the back of the house and the children's bedrooms were at the front. A long hallway was between us. We had gone to bed one night and were just about asleep, when we heard Katie running down the hall. We knew it was her because she usually ran everywhere with small steps, quite different to her brother's slower pace.

"Here comes Katie," Rob said with tired resignation. She was a lively one and often needed a bit of settling at night.

"Mmm," I said, yawning. "I'll take her back."

"It's OK, I'm up now. I'll do it."

Gratefully I snuggled under the blankets. Rob came back quickly and stood at the foot of the bed twirling a piece of hair in the middle of his forehead. He did this when he was puzzled over something or was working on solving a problem. When I first noticed this unique habit, I teased him, saying he was winding up his brain. But tonight he had not been problem-solving.

"Hey, thanks for doing that. Is she settled now?"

"Well, actually, she wasn't up. She's sound asleep in bed."

It took a few moments for the significance of what he was saying to sink in. Then I sprang up, excited, relieved and at the same time nervous about its significance.

"You've heard it too! Oh Rob, you've heard it. That's what I've been hearing for months. Thank God you've heard it too. I can't believe it; at last someone else has heard it."

He slid into bed and hugged me.

"Yes, I did, very clearly, but if it's not Katie, who is it?"

"Remember when I was in hospital the doctor told me that Katie had a twin that did not survive past a couple of months? From what I learnt from Dr McCall, at the moment of conception there is a soul. I explained it all to you when we first met. I wanted to forget about all that. But our little girl, Katie's twin, is asking her mummy and daddy for help. The dear little girl needs our help. Oh Rob, you've heard it because she's your child too."

"But I thought you prayed for her when it happened?"

"Not very thoroughly. I didn't want to think all that stuff was real. It seemed like that experience belonged to the old me, before I knew you. Somehow it seemed quite removed from my new life. I didn't name her, or tell her I loved her. I was quite flippant. I'm so sorry, little one."

As Rob wrapped his soothing arms around me, I cried silently. I heard a whisper coming from outside of myself, but at the same time in the deepest part of me, "*I don't want you to forget.*"

A year before this happened, a friend of mine, John, who was an Anglican minister, was going to England. I had told him of my Aunt Tilly experience and although he did not criticise me, I was not sure that he accepted it either. Just before he left I handed him the name and address of Dr McCall. He told me later that at the time he had just put it in his pocket to be polite, not planning to do anything about it. However, when he arrived in England he realised that he was staying only a mile away from Dr McCall. This, he realised, was more than coincidence. John spent a week with the good doctor, learning about his work. By the time he returned to Australia, he was convinced of the need to develop this ministry.

I phoned John the morning after Rob and I had heard Katie's twin.

"I see," he said soothingly and yet with conviction. "I bet you're relieved that Rob has heard it. It's a real blessing. It makes sense though, as it is his child too."

"You can't imagine how relieved I am. And especially as he's such a scientific, pragmatic man, it adds even more legitimacy to it somehow. Do you know what I mean?"

"Yes, I do," he said with a laugh. "We certainly need to hold a service for her, with you both present."

"Absolutely. Do the children need to come?"

"I don't think that's necessary. I think they would distract you and you really need to be totally present to give attention and love to this child. Have you thought of a name for her?"

"Yes, we thought of a name when this happened. Elise. It means 'consecrated to God'."

"Very appropriate. Unfortunately I have to go away for about ten days but we can hold the service the day after I get back."

After making the arrangements I felt relieved. Very soon we would help our child to move on to where she should be. All that I had experienced and learnt in England was necessary for this very moment.

It seemed like this little child wanted to make sure we did not forget her, because every night we would be woken to the sound of her little footsteps. We also could detect an adult's footsteps. This puzzled us, so we decided to write down anyone we could think of following the guidelines I had learnt from Ken McCall. We started with Rob's family, as I felt I had covered my family. There was nobody there that we could detect. Then we wondered if it was anybody hanging around our house, but after doing a background check, there was nothing extraordinary about its past owners. It was some years later that we realised that the adult's footsteps we were hearing were more than likely our child's guardian angel who is given to everyone to help, guide and protect them during their earthly journey.

The day of the service arrived and Rob and I met with John in a little Anglican chapel. We went through a service designed by Dr McCall in cooperation with sympathetic clergy. During the service we told our daughter that we had named her Elise, and were so sorry we had never had the chance to hold her, to watch her grow and to show her our love. I was flooded with a sensation that could only be described as love. It permeated the small chapel and I imagined little Elise dancing around us gaily, and blowing us kisses, before an angel gently took her by the hand to take her home, to Heaven. This intense feeling was still lingering as we stepped outside into the midday sun. That night and every other night since, all was silent.

Katie never asked for a sister again.

Life settled down and within a few months I had delivered another baby – a boy. With three children under five, it was a happy, lively household. There were not many spare moments or much energy, but this time I could not dismiss what had happened with Elise. Now more than ever I felt I needed to find a place, a spiritual home, in which this experience would be validated and accepted.

It was going to take over 20 years to find.

More seeking

The Baptist Church and the Bible study group had been a good place to be for a few years, but it was as if my soul were craving more. I had many questions about life and faith which could not be answered within their framework of teaching. So we decided to go to a Uniting Church.

About this time Robert had to go overseas for three weeks. Our youngest son was just four months old and was not sleeping very well at night. I was still weak from another caesarean birth and with our two other preschool children there was no time to rest. I found myself walking around in circles, not coping. I fell down on my knees in a desperate prayer to mother Mary. I had no idea why I addressed her, but it felt so good. Even so, I felt heretical and almost blasphemous as my church taught that to give worship to anyone else but God through Jesus is wrong and idolatrous. But I didn't think I was worshipping her, just talking to her like a mother.

My immediate situation engulfed me before I could think much about it. Not long afterwards, I heard about an organisation run by Catholic nuns called the Grey Sisters. I had never heard of them before. They ran a centre that cared for mothers with preschool children who needed a rest and some time out from their usual busy households. In sleep deprived desperation I rang them. A softly spoken woman answered the phone. Without even thinking through what I would say I just blurted out my need.

"I was wondering if it was possible for me and my three children to come and stay for a couple of nights. You see, my husband is away and I'm so tired."

The gentle voice on the other end of the phone explained that they did not have any room at this time. Tears sprang into action and choked my voice as I spluttered, "But I don't know what to feed them for lunch."

The gentle voice on the other end obviously heard my desperation. She asked me to wait for just a minute. Shortly she returned to the phone and said, "Dear, we have made room. You just pack a few things for yourself and come. Don't worry about packing for the children as we have things here for them."

I was relieved to only pack a few things for myself because even that much was almost beyond me. I can still remember with such gratitude how these wonderful nuns scooped up my children when I staggered in, put me to bed and spent the next three days looking after me. The first morning they brought me breakfast in bed. I wept at the loving nurture I was being shown. I was not even a Catholic. From the experience of being with the Baptists who believe that they are obligated to "witness" to the Christian faith, I braced myself for the moment when the nuns would begin to try and convert me. During the three days I was there, they never even hinted at religion, but just went about their work of caring for me and the other women and children. I was reminded of Mother Teresa of Calcutta (Kolkata) wanting to *"be Jesus' hands in the world"*.

When it came time to leave this tranquil, supportive

place, they did not give me a bill, but suggested that I might like to give a donation to their work. After all the child care, food and nurture I had received, this really moved me. It was not a money-making venture but a genuine service of love.

I seriously questioned the teaching of the groups I had been in that said that Catholics were not Christian. In fact, I recalled some quite negative things that had been said about them. The main inference was that they were not Christian and that it was a *real* Christian's responsibility to "save" them.

I had been told that the Catholic Church had beliefs that were "unbiblical", that they worshipped Mary, believed in a place called Purgatory, discouraged people from reading the Bible, and based their salvation on good works rather than by "faith alone". It was only for uneducated people who could easily be manipulated. The Catholic Church, I was told, is actually the Whore of Babylon that is talked about in Revelations and the head of the church, the Pope, is the Antichrist. I had accepted what I was told because other people much more theological than me had said so and there were quotes in the Bible to prove it.

Time moved on and Rob and I went to many Bible study groups and attended a Uniting Church and an Anglican Church. We came across such a diversity of Christian teaching and interpretation. Who was deciding how we should understand a certain passage of Scripture? It seemed that each minister, each Bible study leader was interpreting the Bible in their own way. Often the interpretation from group to group was so varied that I had no idea which one was right. We were also expected to do much of our own research with the use of biblical dictionaries and commentaries.

With little spare time, I wanted someone to tell me definitively what it all meant. Meanwhile the spiritual hunger and restlessness continued to increase.

The beliefs of the last few years began to unravel. I went to church and tried to pray and read the Bible, but it was becoming difficult. It seemed pointless. Although I had been taught that I was "saved" because I had asked Jesus into my life, I did not believe it. There had to be more to it, but I just could not find it. I tried to live a good life, but really what did it matter if I was already going to Heaven? I found going to church on a Sunday morning a chore. Some people told me that I should be at church to give not just to get. But all week I gave out to everyone in my role as a mother, wife, daughter, sister, friend. By the time Sunday came I was worn out being nice and giving. I craved something to fill my hungry soul so that I could continue to be nice and giving. But worshipping Almighty God consisted of singing repetitive praise and worship choruses when my soul was craving something more. Listening to the Bible readings and a sermon was meant to feed my soul, but if the preacher did not deliver anything relevant to me or was a bit boring, I felt empty and dissatisfied. Then every couple of weeks in the Anglican Church we had communion, which was a *symbolic* remembrance of the Last Supper. I came to the conclusion that I could just as easily stay home and read the Bible, pray and even listen to audio tapes of sermons if I wanted to. Gradually I started going less and less, but the hunger in my soul was constant and unrelenting. Seeping up from my heart a question was formulating. Did I have the whole truth or only part of it?

At certain junctions in life, it seems as if circumstances occur that divert us away from familiar paths and onto a new path. In my case this occurred through some very difficult and hurtful events involving an Anglican Church, a curate's wife and a friend. The convergence of these events left me hurt with feelings of betrayal. After being part of this church community for a few years, I had felt comfortable enough to share my "restless spirit" story with a couple of people whom I felt close to. I was still trying to make sense of it all and had hoped these women might be able to help. Unfortunately it all backfired and I was labelled as someone who had wrong theology and was to be excluded from prayer groups and other activities.

Needless to say it was a very difficult time, but from the vantage point of looking back, it was what was necessary to bring me onto the right path. It was like I had been driving down a road that had a few subtle twists and turns but was always heading in the same direction. After being on that road for a long while it felt like I'd suddenly driven headlong into a roadblock with a big sign on it. The crash jarred my body and shook me up badly. The sign I had run into read "end of the road". This is how I felt. I'd had enough of spending my time at a church that still left my spirit hungry and unsettled.

I heard of a short course being run by a Catholic nun in a spirituality centre not far from my home. This nun also did spiritual direction, so once I'd done the course I asked to see her. After a few sessions of sharing my pain of the last year and also wondering why I still felt so spiritually restless, Sister Maria asked if I would share the story that was the cause of so much confusion and alienation.

"Well, I may as well be rejected by the Catholics as well as everybody else," I told her.

As I related the story, Sister Maria sat calmly listening. When I had finished, there was a small pause during which I braced myself for more criticism. Then she said quite nonchalantly, "I don't find anything unusual about that. Catholics have always believed in praying for the dead."

After a stunned silence in which I felt my jaw drop and a my heart beat faster, I exclaimed, "Really! Is that really true?"

Sister Maria nodded.

As the reality of what she just said filtered through my grey cells, I spluttered out a nervous laugh as I exclaimed, "Then maybe I should become a Catholic!"

Sister Maria gave a knowing smile.

But of course this was an impossible consideration. I came from a very anti-Catholic background and I refused to even consider it.

After a while, Sister Maria changed the subject.

"This spiritual restlessness you feel. Do you ever think that it might come from God?"

What a ridiculous thing to suggest, I thought. "Absolutely not! Because of this restlessness I'm alienated from fitting in anywhere in Christian circles. I question everything too much and keep feeling like I need more. Everybody else seems satisfied. I am for a while when we start a new Bible study or something, but then this gnawing begins deep inside me and I just can't satisfy it."

"I would suggest that God is using this feeling to guide you to where you will find the answers to your spiritual hunger."

THE HALF MADE WHOLE

A number of years later, Sister Maria's prophetic words came true.

Surprising discovery

One day, a few months after my conversation with Sister Maria, my mother invited me to accompany her on a day retreat. It was for all denominations and was being held at a beautiful Catholic monastery which stood on top of a small hill surrounded by lush countryside. As we entered the monastery I noticed an article pinned to the door of the church. It disquieted me. The article was about seven Catholic priests who had been working in El Salvador. One after another they had been martyred as they stepped forward to retrieve the Host from the Eucharistic celebration that their tormentors threw on the floor. One priest stepped forward to pick it up and was stabbed to death. The next priest immediately stepped forward to retrieve it and was murdered, then the next and the next until they were all dead. What was so important about that bit of wafer that seven men would choose death, rather than allow it to be thrown on the floor?

It is said that when the student is ready, the teacher will be provided. I was ready and Michaela was there. I met her on this retreat and, guided by my questions, she began to open up the Catholic Church's teaching to me. I was fascinated. She was a "cradle Catholic" and was interested to learn about Protestant Christianity. I was surprised to find that the things she was telling me resonated deeply within my soul.

We went outside to the beautifully lush monastery gardens. It was a mild day and so we sat on the grass as we talked. My first question led immediately to a much longed-for answer.

"Michaela, I'm deeply troubled by that article on the church door about those priests who died while attempting to pick up pieces of wafer off the floor."

"Yes, what faithful men. But of course it wasn't just a wafer."

I looked at her for a moment, puzzled by what she could possibly mean.

"Then what was it?"

"It was Jesus."

I stared at her incredulously, expecting her to wink at me or do something to suggest she was joking. But she looked back at me evenly before she continued.

"When the priest consecrates the wafer, or Host as we call it, Catholics believe that a very mystical thing occurs at that moment." She paused to gauge my reaction before continuing. "Do you recall Jesus talking about us needing to eat his flesh and drink his blood to have life in us?"[8]

"Yes, that's what is said at the communion service, but it's only a metaphor or something."

"That's right. You have bread and wine to remember the death of Jesus. It's a symbolic act."

"Actually, in the Methodist and Baptist Church we used grape juice, because alcohol is perceived as wrong."

"Well, in the Catholic Church we believe that the bread and wine are mystically changed into the body and blood of

---

8   John 6:53–58, 66–67.

Jesus and this is what He said was needed to feed our souls through our earthly life."

"Really? It sounds revolting actually, like cannibalism."

Michaela laughed as she opened a bottle of water and then took a sip while I struggled with the whole concept of this bloody sounding ceremony. And yet she had used the words *feed your soul*. Could this be the missing part to my puzzle?

"So how does it taste?" I finally asked.

"It looks and tastes the same as bread and wine, but we know that it has changed. There have been countless miracles over the centuries in which the bread has actually changed into heart muscle and the wine into drops of blood. It's all been scientifically tested and recorded."[9]

I shifted position on the grass. I was not very comfortable physically or spiritually at this point. "You're kidding. I've never heard of anything like this. Why does it just happen in the Catholic Church?"

"Golly. I've never had to explain all this before. It's difficult to put these profound ideas into words. I think it is because Jesus handed the ability to perform this miracle on to his disciples, who passed it on to the next generation of priests through the ordination rite. It has continued through uninterrupted until this very day. It's called 'apostolic succession'. At the time of the Reformation, when some people broke away from the Catholic Church, this succession was broken. Therefore they were unable to perform the miracle."

I was feeling quite agitated about this concept and yet the excitement at the possibility of its truth was growing in

---

9   *Eucharistic miracles* by Joan Carroll Cruz.

my mind. I needed time to process it all, but before I did, I needed to clarify something.

"Getting back to the body and blood for a moment, it's amazing that anybody would have wanted to do that when Jesus told them about it."

"Absolutely, especially in Jewish society, which had such strict rules about what they could not eat. It's recorded that a lot of Jesus's followers left Him after He had said all that."

"Did they? So what did He do?"

"Nothing. In other places when the people had misunderstood Him with the parables and so on, He actually clarified what He meant. But what He said about His body and blood being true food and drink for the soul He did not call back. What He said was what He meant."[10]

She had said it again. Food for the soul. Was my soul starving for this mystical food, and that was why I felt these "gnawing" hunger-like pains within me?

It sounded very profound and well thought out – a completely different way of understanding this Christian "ritual". Over the ensuing months, I researched this miracle, called "transubstantiation" thoroughly. The more I understood, the more it resonated within me, although the thought of where it was leading also unsettled me.

Over the next few months Michaela and I became good friends as I continually asked her over for another coffee, which meant lots of talking. She also came with many books, which I devoured. I discovered another difference between Catholic and Protestant Christianity when Michaela asked me the question, "Do you base your faith on only the Bible?"

---

10 John 6:66.

"Of course. Isn't that where Jesus left his teachings for us?"

"Actually, He never wrote a book. He left his teachings in the care of the Church."

This was a completely new thought which challenged my theological knowledge. I finished pouring boiling water into my teapot, feeling my emotions beginning to heat up. My first reaction was to defend what I had previously been taught.

"Yes, but the Bible is God's word. It was written under the guidance of the Holy Spirit. I once was taught this verse: *'All Scripture is inspired by God and is profitable for teaching, for reproof, for correction and for training in righteousness ...'*[11] Saint Paul said that. Therefore isn't the Bible the source of Christianity?"

"That's absolutely true," said Michaela gently. "But Saint Paul had to be referring to the Old Testament because the New Testament had not been collated then."

"Not collated? So how did the faith get known before the New Testament was written?" I answered defiantly. I had never considered a time in which Christians did not have a Bible. I brought the teapot covered in its woollen tea-cosy over to the table. Although most people used teabags, I still preferred leaf tea left to draw for a few minutes which allowed the true flavour to seep out.

Patiently Michaela kept expanding my thinking.

"The New Testament was not collated and put in book form until the fourth century. The Jews had the Old Testament, but it was the Church Fathers who kept the faith alive and growing for three and a half centuries before the New Testament was written."

---

11   2 Timothy 3:14–17.

I was experiencing a type of inner panic as the enormity of what this meant filtered through my preconceptions.

It was perplexing to think about passing on this new religion without a book. But if the early Christians did so well without it, why did we need to rely on it so heavily today? I poured out the tea and passed one to Michaela. "So who are the Church Fathers?" I asked her.

"The Church Fathers were men who were not only taught by the 12 apostles, but also were firsthand witnesses to the creation of the Church worldwide. Most, if not all, were martyred by being crucified, beheaded, fed to the lions at the Roman Colosseum, boiled in oil or skinned alive."

"How ghastly!" Michaela's little Pomeranian dog, Tobie, started nuzzling my leg under the table. He'd finished the treat I'd given him and wanted some more. As I walked over to the cupboard to fetch another one, a memory came to me.

"I remember watching movies about the early Christians being thrown to the lions and wondering how you could possibly have a faith so strong that you could do that. I doubt I ever would, let alone being thrown into boiling oil!"

"They were certainly brave men. Anyway they were the ones empowered by the Holy Spirit who personally handed on the oral teaching of Jesus Christ, which preserved and developed the faith."

"So the faith got going and grew well before the New Testament was written? Are any of these men mentioned in the Bible?"

"Yes, actually, one of the great early ones, Saint Clement. I believe he is in the book of Philippians."

Tobie was trying to get my attention again, which was good because it gave me a moment to digest what I was hearing. I pulled out an old ice-cream container from the plastics drawer and filled it with water. While Tobie drank and splashed water on the floor in his haste, I sat down opposite Michaela and said, "I can't believe I've never heard about this before. So how were the people taught without the Bible?"

"By Sacred Tradition."

"Ah, but I remember somewhere, I think it might have been Saint Paul who says something like being aware of false reasoning according to human tradition."[12]

"But this Tradition isn't based on any erroneous human traditions. Rather it's the deposit of divine truths that Jesus orally entrusted to his apostles, which are not explicitly contained in the Bible."

I drank the last sip of tea and placed the cup down slowly into its saucer.

"So what's happened to Sacred Tradition now that we have the Bible?"

"Catholics use the two together. To attempt the interpretation of Scripture without recourse to Tradition would be like performing a surgical operation on a corpse."

As I listened intently to all that Michaela was saying, my mind whizzed around as if it were in a blender, the blades cutting violently through my previous belief system. But I was also feeling excited by what she was saying, as many of my own doubts and questions were answered. I had just assumed that I was an odd person lacking in some personal quality that enabled me to become compliant with the teachings and beliefs of the various churches I had attended. Despite desperately wanting to believe, the inner hunger and longing would not abate and so I kept searching. But now it was like I was unravelling a puzzle. Many pieces of

---

12 Colossians 2:8.

this puzzle had been missing while other pieces seemed stranded in a bottom drawer unable to find a place to fit. I needed to find all the pieces so I kept asking questions and read a variety of spiritual books.

Over yet another morning coffee, this time at her house, I was ready with some more questions for Michaela.

"Does the Catholic Church teach the same things? I've attended a number of different Protestant denominations and I've found just as many varying interpretations. I was never sure which one had it right."

"Yes, it does," answered Michaela as she carried some yummy homemade biscuits to the table. "All the teachings are compiled in a book called the Catechism."

I had found the Bible to be a rich source of wisdom and teaching, but from my experience it is a difficult book to understand and interpret. I came across a verse in the Bible that confirmed my thinking.

"There are some things in all (Paul's) letters that are hard to understand, which the ignorant and unstable twist to their own destruction, as they do the other Scriptures."[13]

In the books I was reading it explained the use of the Bible within the Catholic Church. It was not left up to personal interpretation, as most people throughout the centuries would have been ignorant of the historical context or the symbolism used in biblical times. Therefore, if not understood properly, the passage could mean something quite different today from the writer's intention. The original teachings were handed down from the Church Fathers who made sure the real meanings were preserved and taught. Further explanations were passed down with

---

13 2 Peter 3:16.

the oral Traditions that were as carefully preserved as the written texts. It was quite a revelation to realise that there was more to the Christian faith than just the Bible alone. Here was a verse that I had never noticed before.

"But there are also many things which Jesus did; were every one of them to be written, I suppose that the world itself could not contain the books that would be written."[14]

It was like I was diving to the bottom of a deep ocean filled with valuable pearls, whereas up until now I had been paddling in the shallows. There was one particular topic that I needed to discuss with Michaela and so I arranged to meet with her yet again. As it was a sunny morning, we decided to go for a walk down by the upper end of the Yarra River close to where Michaela lived. There had been some decent rain recently so the river was quite full and flowing rapidly. It was like walking through the countryside and yet we were only about 27 kilometres from the city. It seemed like a good time to test my new friendship.

"I'm going to share with you a couple of incidents from my past. Some people have found them scary and heretical, but I keep mentioning them hoping to find a satisfactory theological home for them."

So I shared my experiences of the restless spirit of my aunt Tilly and also of Katie's twin sister. Michaela listened intently, her eyes filling with tears as I told her about the little twin. I was feeling anxious in the event that she would discount it all as a figment of my imagination or as a trick of the devil or similar.

"That's so beautiful!" Michaela said, wiping her eyes. "I think you have been given a wonderful gift to help you to understand. Catholics from the very beginning have

---

14 John 21:5.

prayed for their dead. We even devote a special day for it in November called All Souls' Day. Most people need some time after they die to be fully purified to reach Heaven."

I looked with amazement at Michaela, unable to say very much at the implications of what she had just said. Finally I was able to ask in a voice that sounded like a whisper, "Where are these people then, if they are dead but not in Heaven?"

"Let's start back a bit. Why don't we sit on this bench. I often sit here just to watch the waterbirds on the river. I believe we are on earth to prepare ourselves to live with God in Heaven. But it has also been taught that 'nothing unclean can enter Heaven'."[15]

"But didn't Jesus's death allow us to go to Heaven even though we don't deserve it?"

"By His death the gates of Heaven were reopened after they had been closed when man began to disobey God right at the beginning of humankind. But it doesn't necessarily mean we can just get in."

"Even if we believe in Him and ask Him into our lives?" I felt I was getting close to the answer I had been looking for and yet it was systematically dispersing my previously held ideas.

"The thing is," continued Michaela, "everybody has been *redeemed*, even those who have never heard of Jesus. But everybody has to work out their own *salvation* with fear and trembling, as one of the disciples says."[16]

I watched a little egret with its legs trailing behind it fly gracefully to a tree stump on the edge of the river.

"So it takes more than just accepting Jesus into our life?"

---

15 Revelation 21:27.
16 Philippians 2:12.

"Yes. We need to work at becoming more perfect and holy."[17]

"And if we are not, at that point when we die?"

"We are given an enormous grace from God who allows us a time of purification."

"Is this what Ken McCall referred to as 'no man's land'?"

"Historically it is referred to as Purgatory, which comes from the verb 'to purge', meaning to purify or cleanse. It is a temporary state and everyone who gets to Purgatory will make it to Heaven."

This was making sense, although it sounded like another sort of Christianity to the one I had learnt about. The little egret ducked its head under the water and caught a small fish in its long pointed bill. We both cheered the beautiful bird for catching its lunch. The sun was right above us now, causing the river to glisten even more. It was such a tranquil setting for this memorable chat. Michaela, perceiving that I was very interested, continued on.

"We can help our friends and relatives move through this time of cleansing by praying."

"Oh my goodness. That is what Aunt Tilly was asking me to do for her!" I noticed my hands had become sweaty as I hung on every word with great anticipation.

"That's what I'm getting to. It has been known in many documented cases for God to allow a person to visit a relative to ask them for prayers. In fact, in the book of Maccabees we are told to pray for our dead."[18]

"Ah, now, this is the thing," I said, feeling apprehensive as I did not want to stop this way of thinking, but had to

---

17 Matthew 5:48.
18 2 Maccabees 12:46.

make sure everything was clarified. "In the Bible I have studied we don't have the book of Maccabees."

"As I understand it, seven books were taken out of the Bible at the time of the Reformation because they were contrary to Martin Luther's theology."

I was very impressed with Michaela's understanding of Catholic theology and of her ability to explain it so clearly. But more importantly I recognised that at long last my restless spirit experience had found a theological home. We turned away from the river and headed back along the bush track to her home. I recognised a bounce in my step and a lightness in my heart.

Following this enlightening talk, I began to read about the theology of Purgatory. Surprisingly it was mentioned very many times in the Bible, in passages that I had skimmed over before and never understood their true meaning.[19] Finally someone, on behalf of the Catholic Church, had validated my experience, which had confused me and caused feelings of alienation for over 20 years. I began to devour books and read many articles on the web as well as talking it over with my friend. My theological horizons were expanding as I drank in this new theology.

Then one day I received a phone call from Rob, which would put an end to these stimulating times with Michaela.

---

19 Matthew 12:32, 1 Corinthians 3:5, 1 Peter 3:18–20, 1 Peter 4:6, 2 Timothy 1:16–18, 1 Corinthians 15:29–30.

Root loosening

"Hi, honey. Are you sitting down?" Rob asked me as he rang from his office.

"Oh dear, this sounds ominous," I said, easing into the nearest chair.

"How would you like to live in America for a couple of years?"

Within a few months we had packed up our home and three teenagers and went to live in a regional town in Ohio. I was confused about why God would take me away just when I was beginning to find some answers to my spiritual questions. I had never mixed with Catholics before Michaela, especially as I had been brought up in a strictly Protestant household that was actually against Catholicism. I expected that the move to America was going to end my spiritual search in this area. But I was to realise in the following years that this move was an integral part of my spiritual journey.

In this town, set amidst beautiful cornfields and wide rivers, I had the space to explore the Catholic faith without negative pressure from extended family and other well-meaning friends. Interestingly, I kept meeting Catholics, which I saw as providential. Then one day I met a young priest in a bookshop. Without Michaela, I had no one to talk to about the things I was discovering. After I asked him some questions in the shop, Father Frank invited me to come and speak with him whenever I had any other questions. So every two or three weeks I would journey down the busy Interstate 75 to Cincinnati where I could talk over with him all the things I was learning.

I also met Corey who had converted to the Catholic faith a few years earlier. Her husband was an officer in the navy and they had moved around every few years. Therefore she had begun homeschooling her children to provide them with continuity in their studies. A number of years earlier she had searched around for a homeschooling curriculum. Surprisingly she found the Catholic curriculum to be the most comprehensive. Through this she began to understand and became interested in the Catholic faith and before long she decided to convert. This equipped her with invaluable knowledge and the perspective to teach me more about the faith.

During the first 18 months of being in Ohio, I fully researched the Catholic faith. The more I understood, the more my preconceived ideas about Catholicism were dismantled. I realised they had been based on ignorance. More astonishingly, I discovered that I had previously only known part of the Christian religion. The part I had known was the Christian faith after Martin Luther had modified it in the 15th century. Since that time many people had moved further away from the original religion as they developed their own interpretations of Christianity. Within America alone I found there were 30,000 different Protestant denominations.

After visiting Father Frank for about a year, I was sitting in my usual chair telling him of yet another spiritual insight, when he smiled at me and said calmly, "You know, Julie, you've been a Catholic in your heart for many years, but it is only recently that you have put it together in your head. It's like you have been putting pieces of a jigsaw puzzle together."

I looked at him in horror, my heartbeat accelerating. After a stunned pause I whispered, "Do you mean I should become a Catholic?"

"Well, I think you already are in your heart."

My voice increased in volume and pitch as I blurted out, "But I couldn't take that step; I mean, my family back home would kill me! Not literally, of course, but it would cause terrible friction and bad feeling. I'm not sure I could do it."

Father Frank was probably wondering why I had been coming to talk with him for the last 12 months. But I had enjoyed finding answers to lifelong questions and felt spiritually alive and mentally invigorated. For some reason during all this time I had never actually considered becoming Catholic. The idea was far too intimidating.

Plunging into the Tiber

As I drove home down the interstate, my mind was in turmoil. To become Catholic would mean moving away culturally from my husband, children and extended family, as well as many friends. I knew it would be particularly upsetting to my mother, and had my father been alive, he would have been even more upset. He had been very involved in the Masonic Lodge, as had my grandfathers and uncles. The Lodge, I knew, was very anti-Catholic. This sentiment was a religious bias that was much more pronounced in previous generations than in my own, it seemed. But the hunger in my soul had been driving me on to find truth for years and in my mind over the last couple of years I had found it. How could I ignore that?

By the time I arrived home, I had reached a decision. Calling my husband and children together, I asked them how they would feel if I were to become a Catholic. I tried to explain what that would mean.

"It would not be right away. Actually, I would have to go through a nine-month course called the Rite of Christian Initiation for Adults (RCIA), which is a course that teaches you everything about being Catholic. You can pull out at any time if you don't agree with or like the teaching."

"Go for it, Mum."

"Yeah, Mum, it's OK with us, if that's what you want."

"For most of our married life you have been spiritually discontent and restless. Over the last couple of years I can tell you have found something. So if you think this is the way, you should go, I'll support you."

It was an unexpected green light from the people in my life that my decision would have the most impact on.

"Thank you, my darlings," I said, embracing them all in one of our united family hugs. I was especially touched by Rob's generous attitude.

Everything was in place for me to begin the journey to enter the Catholic Church. A requirement of doing the RCIA[20] program was to have a companion more mature in the faith to walk the journey with you. This person is called a sponsor and I had the perfect person to be mine.

Every week Corey and I would drive to a town about half an hour away in her bright green VW beetle. The beautiful countryside changed from deep greens in the summer to bright orange and maroon in autumn to a white fairyland in the winter snow. We had the most invigorating talks on our journeys. The more I learnt in the lessons, the more I was convinced that this was where I was meant to be.

I finally decided to let my mother and sister know of my decision. Although Anne had been to visit us for a few weeks and we had talked about my journey, at that time I was not contemplating joining the Church. When I emailed

---

20   RCIA stands for Rite of Christian Initiation for Adults. This is a nine-month program which is about Formation – it provides information about what the Catholic Church teaches, and why she does so, but it is also about human formation. It introduces those people who are interested into the life and love of the Church. The RCIA process seeks to prepare people not merely for assent to eternal truths, but more so to fall in love with an eternal Lover.

them with the news of my upcoming confirmation into the Catholic Church, my poor mother was furious, although I think it was more a combination of fear and a sense of family betrayal on my part. Anne was also cross.

"Honestly, Julie," she said one evening during one of her many phone calls in which she tried to dissuade me. "Catholicism is for ignorant people who are superstitious. You'd be going backwards on your spiritual journey." I think she really believed this, but I also knew she felt me becoming increasingly separated from her.

My mother decided to give me the silent treatment as an indication of her disapproval, hoping, I supposed, to jolt me back to my senses. I did find it difficult and yet this reaction was not unexpected. We had always been a family who were honest with each other and didn't hold things back when we disagreed. I think we could do that because we were sure of each other's undeniable love which we knew would never waver. My older brother supported me so much through this difficult time. We had always been close, and he knew the struggles I had experienced as a twin. He perceptibly saw this decision not only as a spiritual decision, but also as a giant step towards my individuality.

On a crisp moonlit night on the Saturday evening before Easter, with my dear family to witness it, I was confirmed into the Catholic Church. It was a type of church service that we as a family had never experienced. It was profound and mystical. Afterwards Rob came over to kiss me and I will never forget his first words to me.

"Boy. We've been messing around in kindergarten up until now, haven't we?"

It has been over 15 years now since I entered the Catholic Church. The inner hunger and emptiness left immediately and has never returned. I had been led to my spiritual home. Sister Maria's words proved absolutely correct.

Five months after this night, the new RCIA program was about to begin. I asked Rob if he would be interested in attending some of the classes to understand more about the Church that I was now a part of. He decided that he would attend just a few lessons. After a month of weekly classes I expected him to stop, but he kept going for another month. The priest and the deacon who ran the classes were extremely well educated and knew a great deal about church history. They were able to answer intelligently the many questions that were asked. Deacon Bob lent Rob a book, which he began to read that very night.[21] One evening when Rob was about halfway through this book, he had a moment of epiphany. From then on he was convinced that the Catholic Church contained the fullness of the Christian faith. The following Easter he also entered the Church. During this time our daughter had been going out with a young man who began taking her to his church's youth group. There Katie became friends with the youth worker, Christie. Christie answered Katie's questions and gradually taught her the Catholic faith. A few months after Rob, Katie also entered the Catholic Church.

---

21 *Short history of the Catholic Church* by Phillip Hughes.

Terrorism in America

Following this very significant time, I had peace in my soul for perhaps the first time in my life. The restlessness had gone and Rob and I were once again on the same faith path which felt like a spiritual honeymoon. We now had a place to go to receive food for our souls and many other spiritual graces that God bestows through His Church's Sacraments. We were going to need this spiritual strength in the weeks ahead and even more so in events to come in the next few years.

Deciding to move to America with our three children was difficult, especially considering an incident in one of the schools a few months before we arrived. In Colorado State, two senior students from Columbine High School went on a shooting spree, killing 12 fellow students and a teacher, as well as injuring 24 others. With the legacy of this event permeating the school system, and with much trepidation, we placed our three teenage children into the American high school system. Each morning they had to walk through a metal detector, and instead of running around outside at lunchtime, everyone had to stay inside all day. The doors to the outside were locked in an attempt to prevent any assassins from entering. Still, guns were easily obtainable in America. As we discovered, the Americans had a different view to most Australians on owning personal weapons. They adhered to the words of one of their former presidents, Thomas Jefferson.

"No free man shall ever be debarred the use of arms."

The strongest reason for people to retain their right to keep and bear arms is as a last resort to protect themselves against tyranny in government.

The American people on the whole thought that while gun laws should make a country a safer place to live, in reality they are a move against the freedom and self-defence of the people. Therefore guns could quite easily be purchased.

Following the massacre at Columbine High School, the gun lobby ran a scare campaign on television showing graphic footage of guns being destroyed in Australia under Prime Minister Howard's new gun policy following the massacre of 35 people in the sleepy tourist town of Port Arthur, Tasmania. In a matter of weeks after the Port Arthur massacre, the Australian government passed legislation to remove semi-automatic weapons from the Australian population, and a "gun buy-back" proceeded. It is now illegal to own any semi-automatic gun in Australia. This initiative has been used by the American gun lobby as a deterrent to changing the American gun laws. They perceive it as the government taking away the rights of individuals to defend their freedom.

Despite the fear I felt, our children settled well into school and adjusted to the very different system. It did, however, take them a while to be comfortable with being locked inside all day. After a couple of years, our family had settled into the beautiful rural area of Ohio, going about our normal daily lives. Then on a very ordinary autumn morning, America was attacked by Muslim extremists. As the planes flew into the New York Twin Towers and the Pentagon in Washington DC, Americans went into shock.

That morning I had taken my daughter to see a doctor in Cincinnati about 90 kilometres from our home town. I also had a friend from Australia staying with us. As we came out of the doctor's room we saw the receptionists behind the desk were quite distraught.

"A plane has just flown into one of the Twin Towers in New York. I can't believe it. I was only there a month ago and I was in that tower," said one of them.

"What was wrong with the plane?" I asked.

"They don't know yet. Must have been a mechanical failure," replied the other receptionist.

Having planned to stop off at a shopping mall on the way home, we headed off along Interstate 75. As we walked inside this usually busy place we were surprised to find it almost deserted. Walking further we saw a group of people huddled around a television.

"What's going on?" I said.

A rather big man who had red eyes and looked pale answered me, his voice punctuated with sobs, "Another plane has just gone into the second tower. America is under attack!"

Needless to say, this put an end to our shopping trip. We immediately headed for home back along the interstate. To reach our town we passed by numerous exits into other towns. As we drove by the exits leading into the city of Dayton, we saw they were blocked off with portable gates and big signs on which was written in bold red print "Closed". I knew that a big United States Air Force base was situated in Dayton and wondered if they were concerned that it might be a target. (I was to find out later that this is what they had predicted.)

I was feeling agitated and just wanted to get home quickly. We had the car radio on, listening intently to the news, and I pressed my foot harder on the accelerator when it was reported that yet another plane had crashed, this time into the Pentagon in Washington DC, the nation's capital. The attacks seemed to be accelerating and were quite unpredictable. The children were sent home from school as nobody knew what was going to happen. We stayed glued to the television for hours as we watched in horror as desperate people jumped out of the Twin Towers rather than being burned alive. Then when the towers came crashing down we helplessly watched the terrible scenes of distressed and injured people trying to escape the massive dust cloud that chased after them. When the news came through that yet another plane had come down in a field in Pennsylvania, the feelings of foreboding accelerated. The media reported that it was thought the passengers on Flight 93 may have manoeuvred the crash to stop the plane from hitting its target. It was suspected that this plane had been hijacked to fly into the Capitol Building in Washington DC, the icon of American democracy.

In the following days an air of disbelief and grief permeated our stunned town. Many of the people I spoke to asked the same question.

"Why doesn't the world like us?"

Family back home continued to phone, wondering if we should return to Australia, but as all the aeroplanes within America had been grounded, nobody could enter or leave the country. It was over a week before the planes started flying again and it took months for people to feel confident to fly. Not that we intended to leave America. We felt a connection to our adopted country of the last couple of years and felt their pain. American flags went up in every house either on makeshift flagpoles or on front windows. One day everybody was asked to wear red, white and blue as a symbol of camaraderie and patriotism.

On the following weekend our town, Troy, population 23,000, held a memorial service. At least half that number turned up in the town square where various churches had prepared a sombre, heartfelt service. As the sun set on the chilly autumn evening, we all lit a candle. The large crowd was subdued and very quiet. Each church leader gave a short message of encouragement, while acknowledging the hurt and bewilderment of the American people. There was a camaraderie shared that evening as the people stood side by side, immersed in a collective grief. Only the occasional quiet whimper or nose blow disturbed the peace.

Then a short man, who was the minister of one of the 27 church denominations in our town, strode to the centre of the stage and with a voice tinged with anger yelled into the microphone completely dissipating the stillness.

"America you have deserved this! Your sins have brought the wrath of God down upon our land!"

He spoke like this for a number of minutes, his speech periodically interjected by some of his parishioners, dotted strategically around the crowd, as they cried out with hands in the air:

"Yes, Lord."

"That's right. Alleluia."

"Yes, Lord. Praise His name forever!"

Everybody was too stunned to react. We just sat placidly absorbing the accusations and the image of a vengeful God.

When he finally sat down, nobody moved. After a significant time the Anglican minister walked slowly across the stage and rang a deep melodious bell three times. Everybody sat quietly, some patting their tear-filled eyes as the sound of the bell reverberated through the now dark night. Gradually people got up, folded their chairs and departed without speaking.

As they walked past the American flag in the middle of the city square, they paused and saluted or put their hand on their chest like they do when they sing the national anthem. But the flag, which usually flew proudly, was tonight hanging limply as if it too was in mourning.

Over the ensuing weeks it was noted that many people flowed into the churches. Maybe people acknowledged their inner need to respond to God when things happen in life over which they have no control. Maybe they wanted to find answers to the big question of suffering. Maybe they wanted to support Christianity over Islam when it became apparent who was behind the attacks. Maybe they wanted to pray for those who were killed and for protection from pending danger.

One thing was obvious. When an event happens that is beyond people's ability to control, they instinctively look for something or someone greater than themselves to which to turn. Why people suffer is a big question and one that I had often pondered on. In my younger days I had considered the idea of karma, in which suffering came to you as a result of what you had done either in the life you were living or from one of your previous lives. As a Protestant, I encountered a number of explanations. The predominant idea was that if you experienced suffering it was because you were not praying correctly or asking for God's protection and guidance. If you remained consistent in prayer and reading of the Scriptures then He would bless you with success in all your undertakings. Therefore, I thought that if things went wrong, then I was in some way responsible.

But when I explored Catholic theology, I was introduced to a completely different idea of suffering. I read about many people who maintained their peace and joy in the midst of terrible suffering, even thanking God for what they were enduring. This reminded me of what Saint Paul had said in Asia Minor when he was imprisoned and which I had always wondered about.

"*Now I rejoice in my sufferings for your sake and in my flesh I complete what is lacking in Christ's afflictions for the sake of his body, that is the Church.*"[22]

I struggled with this idea that any good could come out of pain and suffering, but slowly I grasped a new way of thinking about it and it made more sense to me.

"*Suffering is indeed a mystery. Yet through faith, the Christian can discover in the darkness of his own or other people's suffering, the loving and provident hand of his Father God who knows so much more and sees so much farther than he himself can … Obviously God wants us to avoid pain and illness with all the means at our disposal, but at the same time when suffering does come that it can have a redemptive meaning and lead to our own personal purification, even in the case of those which seem unjust or out of proportion.*"[23]

It will probably take a lifetime to grasp the full depth of this theology about suffering, but I understood enough to change the question from "why should I suffer?" to "what shall I do *when* I suffer?" This was an important distinction

---

22 Colossians 1:4.
23 *In conversation with God* by Francis Fernandez.

in the way I approached life in the future, especially when faced with what was in store for me in the next few years.

Gradually America began to heal from the terrorist attack and people returned to their normal lives. The planes flew again but the airports would never be the same. Precautions were put in place with luggage and personal searches that caused delays and huge queues, which was a constant reminder of how "dangerous" the authorities thought plane travel had become.

Our family had initially gone to America for two years but we stayed for four. We look back on these years as one of the highlights of our family life with all the adventures we had and the wonderful people we met. It gave us a greater sense of our Australian identity as we experienced the differences in our cultures.

Returning home proved to be a huge adjustment. People said that it is easier to settle into a new country than it is to return home. I had rejected this idea as nonsense. How could it be difficult to return home to your own house and neighbourhood, friends and family? You would just pick up where you left off, wouldn't you?

Well, actually, they were right. I had not considered how living offshore can change you. Experiences had changed my world view and theological perspective. Life moves on for everyone and without common experiences you discover that with some friendships you no longer connect in a way that is mutually satisfying. Some friends journey with you through life and I have been blessed to have a number of these special people in my life. But other friendships are only for a period of time, when it is mutually affirming and beneficial, and when the time is right they just fizzle out. But before new friendships are made, it can be a lonely time.

Compounding these feelings was the fact that Rob had to return to America for four months to finish his contract.

Then out of the blue, or that's how it seemed, "middle-agedness" swooped with a vengeance. The deluge of emotions as my hormones plummeted had a dramatic effect and I struggled to keep my usual cheerful attitude. As the months and years went by, I felt like I was being sucked into a dark cave full of fear and sadness. I struggled against it with mental acrobatics and my new-found faith. I wanted life to come to a halt for a while so that my mind and heart could catch up with the rapid changes that had taken place and were still taking place in my life.

My daughter Katie had married and given birth to a darling little daughter within two years of coming home, so now I was a grandmother. My eldest son had moved to another state for work and my youngest son was quickly developing his independence, which is what good parenting encourages. But everything had changed so quickly.

An intense feeling of redundancy chased by depression descended and sucked me deeper into the dark cave. Thinking that I needed another focus, I started a job. A friend opened the way for me to work in a hospital as a unit receptionist. I had never done this sort of work before, but the personnel lady assured me that I would catch on fast. I liked the idea of moving into the workforce again, but instead, it increased the stress as I worked hard at mastering the various computer programs and fitting in with the hospital culture.

To compound it all I was on the "bank system", which meant I went to different wards all over the hospital, each with their own way of doing things. I kept hoping that I would begin to feel better, but with my attempt to find a new purpose in life I was making things worse.

Then one day I had another phone call from Robert.

"They've asked me to take a position in Shanghai."

The next day I resigned from the job and began planning for the new adventure, thinking that this would be just the thing to help me find a new purpose and help lift the suffocating feelings that I had not been able to shift. Three months later we arrived in China.

Infants Julie (L) Anne (R)

Toddlers Julie(L) Anne (R)

1974 Julie dances with lady in Papua New Guinea village

1975 Julie on her motor bike in Alice Springs

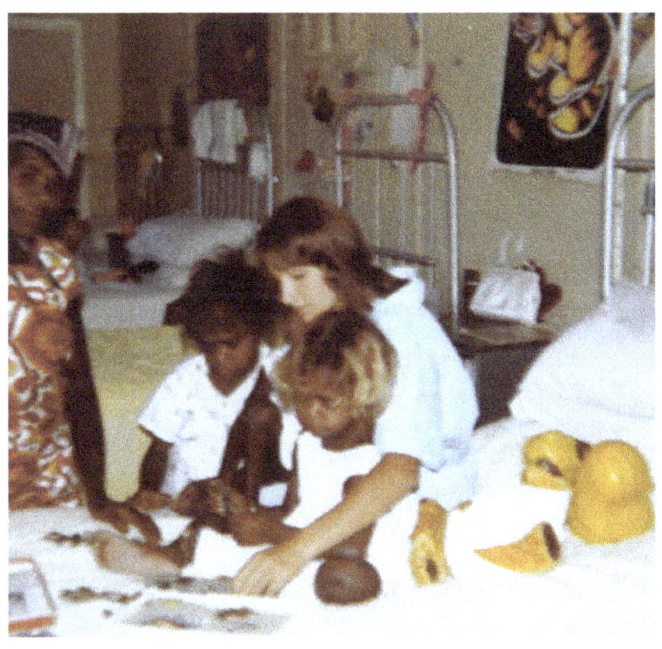

Working with Aboriginal children in the local hospital

Kayaking in the Southern Ocean in Tasmania 1973

1981…Julie as bride and Anne as her bridesmaid

1981 Robert and Julie

1994 The young family. Katrina, Peter and Stephen

2004 Julie and Anne on Katrina's wedding day

2008 With shop keeper in China

2007 Dancing in China at company dinner

Mid-life in the Middle Kingdom

The Chinese word for China is "Zhong Goren", which means The Middle Kingdom.

The black dog bites

I was 52 years old when we moved to China. Of course, it did not turn out to be for the two years the contract stated, but once again stretched out to four years. Looking back I realise that I needed the extra time to let our life in China teach us its lessons. It became a symbiotic meeting of place and person, the right time to gather together the heterogeneous threads of life and reflect upon them.

It was early March when we arrived and still bitterly cold, with grey skies and particularly freezing winds that blew down from Russia going right through to our bones. It took until the next winter to learn that only a duck-down coat keeps you warm in these temperatures. But for this winter our woollen coats did not help much and left us shivering when we ventured out. The crowded streets were damp and grey while the weak winter sun could barely infiltrate the smoggy sky.

We arrived on a Saturday evening and on Monday morning Rob left for work. I stood in the middle of the hotel room wondering what on earth I was going to do. I did not know where to go to buy food and did not as yet understand the currency. The few people I ran into could not speak English and I did not know any Chinese. In time, of course, I made friends, learnt some Mandarin and could navigate my way around. But initially it was overwhelming, and instead of subsiding, the feelings that I had experienced back home only became more and more intense. I felt like I was now in the centre of the dark sad cave.

I look back on the early weeks in China like another person watching a replay of scenes in a movie.

In one scene it was early afternoon in Shanghai and the sun was hiding behind grey skies. The winter trees looked dead and the tops of the tall buildings were hidden under low clouds that looked murky as they mingled with the pollution. If you stood at the foot of the building called Times Square on Middle Huai Hai Road and looked up 18 floors to the double windows, you might have been able to see a tiny speck of a woman.

This was me. I gazed out absently onto the bustling megacity, watching the millions of people, bikes and cars moving with purpose towards their millions of different activities.

The vastness of it diminished me. I felt smaller than the speck you might have seen in the window. For the first time in my life I had nowhere to go and nothing fulfilling to do. The last 25 years in particular, when I devotedly spent my time as a mother and housewife, were gone. This left a vacuum in my life that I had no idea how to fill. So I stood at the window, forehead leaning against the glass, arms hanging limply, shoulders slightly hunched, trying to control the rising sense of redundancy and its unwelcome partner, depression, which were pressing down and around me as if I were in a vice that was squeezing all the life out of me. Looking down, the thought again entered my head. How easy it would be to just open the window less than a metre, put one leg through, and then the other until …

Only the previous week the local newspaper had reported that a window washer in this same district of Luwan had plunged to his death from one of these buildings. It saddened me to see these migrant workers from rural China, who had probably never been in a dwelling higher than a single storey, working as window washers on these skyscrapers. Most days you could look at any high building and see them balanced on small wooden boards with a rope threaded through, on which they sat, a bucket of water attached to one side, arms stretched out with window scrapers and rags, washing the grime off the windows of this massive city. They would do something to the rope and, *whoosh*, they dropped to the next storey. Without help from scaffolding or cherry pickers, the men dangled on tenuous ropes from the sky. A few times I had seen them right outside my window. I held my breath and waited for them to move safely down to the next floor, afraid that one day I might see a body tumbling past the window, a frayed rope trailing behind it.

The normal adjustments to living in a new country that I had usually found exciting and stimulating were instead swamping me. I felt like my emotional resilience was seeping out. The mental and spiritual strength that I had developed during my life and that had always allowed me to cope seemed elusive, although I had a deep sense that I was not really alone, that I should be watchful to observe the little rays of light that would filter through into my dark sad cave.

In the meantime, during the afternoons I had to shut the world out. So, I closed all the curtains to block out the city, grabbed a soft blanket and headed for the couch. I curled up tightly, knees resting just under my chin as I gently rocked back and forth, like I used to rock my babies for comfort. I reached out for some tissues to wipe away the tears that had begun again and were dropping onto the cushion under my head, leaving round, damp patches. Normally a good cry is what a person needs to shift grief or release frustration or hurt feelings, and when the pain subsides the tears will stop. But these tears did not stop. They just kept going and going. A number of times I needed to call Life Line, which had opened a branch in Shanghai, just to talk to someone to help me stop crying.

Years ago I used to work as a counsellor on Life Line in Melbourne, never considering that one day I would be on the other end.

"How can I help you?" asked the counsellor, with an American accent.

I couldn't answer straight away as a sob, heavy with despair, was blocking my throat.

"I, I … I can't stop crying," I finally said, exhaling.

"Can you tell me why you are crying?" She sounded genuine.

"I'm just so sad."

"Do you know why?"

"No … well, everything. I feel like … oh my mind is whirling, it feels so … I feel like my life may as well be over. I'm redundant!" Another heavy sob had worked its way through, making my voice high and quavering.

"How long have you felt like this?"

I was finding it hard to talk, so I covered the mouthpiece of the phone and let out another sob. It took a few more seconds until I could breathe in and talk.

"A couple of years … although it has got worse since we came here."

"Did you want to come to China?"

"Well, yes, I did. When my husband was offered the position here, I thought it would be a good adventure and help snap me out of the sadness. I've always loved travel and exploring other cultures. But this time I'm not. It's all too much."

"Have you managed to make any friends here?"

"Yes, I've met some great ladies who are very friendly. I usually enjoy meeting new people, but now it's such an effort."

"Does anyone know how you feel?"

"No. I put on my happy mask. New friends don't want to have sad people around. I mean, this is not me. I'm not normally like this. But I don't want people to see me like this. I don't like me like this."

"That must be difficult for you."

"It exhausts me, actually. I'm thinking that I may have lost myself somewhere along the way. I feel like a shell, an empty shell." I shut my eyes and breathed in deeply. "Thank you for talking to me. I've stopped crying now."

"You're welcome, but please call back if you need to."

I hung up the phone and returned to the couch. Picking up the remote control I turned on the television, hoping this was a day when the satellite was working. Robert was away for the week and the afternoon and evening kept stretching out further and further. I should go for a walk, do some shopping or have a foot massage, I thought. But the darkened room was like my cocoon. I needed to strengthen my inner wings to leave it. I settled for numbing my mind with constant movies. To hasten the process I opened a bottle of wine, poured a glass and left the bottle on the side table within easy reach.

The movie was half over, but I had seen it before. It was about a man whose daughter was getting married. He found it so hard to let her go as they had been so close.

I could identify with the father. Twenty-four years ago, when I became pregnant with my first child, I stepped out of my career, always assuming that I would return to it. But another child followed and then another, in quick succession. My whole world view changed as I discovered that mothering was more than a full-time job. It took every bit of mental and physical capacity to be the best mother I could be. Even then I hadn't recovered from the wonder of bringing three children into the world and the thrill of watching them develop. And I was experiencing it again as a grandmother, but at a distance of 10,000 kilometres.

I took a big gulp of wine. It was not good wine, rather bitter.

Thoughts were rushing around my head like two voices battling for supremacy.

Voice A: "I always wanted to be a mother and a wife, to create a peaceful home for everyone."

Voice B: "That really was an archaic attitude. It was OK in the 1950s or earlier, but this is the 21st century. Women do more than just that!"

Voice A: "But I didn't have the capabilities to do this and keep up my career at the same time."

Voice B: "Was that really my thoughts or was it the influence of that fundamental Christian sect that I was involved in at the time? The one that taught that mothers should not work and should be submissive to their husbands."

Voice A: "Maybe that might have been part of it initially,

but I didn't know how I could leave my little children in a crèche all day."

Voice B: "But it would have been fine. Most kids are left at crèches even if only for a couple of days to give the mums a break."

Voice A: "I should have. I wish I had kept up my career. I wish I had not seen my family as the absolute priority. What an idiot I am. They're all fine, off living their own lives, standing well on their own. My husband has had a wonderful career life. What have I achieved with my life? What am I going to do now? I'm so stupid and short sighted. Why didn't I see that this would happen?"

Voice B: "I'm too old to start again. I've let all my work skills go, I'm so redundant."

The father in the movie stood waving to his daughter as she drove off from the wedding. He had a peaceful smile on his face as he put an arm around his wife and drew her close. He rested his head on top of hers and whispered with contented resignation, "Well, it's just you and me again now, darling."

Putting the empty wine glass on the table, I lay down. I did not want it to be just myself and Robert, because when he went away, as he often did in his work, there was no one. I had never been totally on my own before. I wished I could just go to sleep.

Being alone for a while was solitude, a time out from the demands of others. But when it was for days and weeks, it was lonely. Some people flourished being by themselves. Robert enjoyed it. He was happy to tinker away on one project or another, ride his bike around or get involved in other solitary pursuits not needing company. In fact, often he preferred to be alone. He said he dealt enough with people at work. But being alone like this was frightening for me. I felt more panicky the longer it went on. Someone had said to me a while ago that I may just have to learn to be alone. But how does a person who has always had company, even since conception where I shared the womb with my twin sister, learn that?

Normally I would have tried to have the week booked up with interesting and fun things to do with a variety of friends. But the way I was feeling I couldn't find the impetus to organise anything, or even to make a phone call. Nothing seemed interesting to do anyway.

"Oh God," I thought, and prayed. "How will I ever be happy again? How do I get used to being on my own? What is my purpose in life now?"

As I threw the blanket back over my head, I think God silently and with a smile tucked me up, because He knew, even though I did not know it at the time, that I had already begun the journey on which these three desperate questions were going to be answered.

The first thread

A few weeks later I once again stood at the window of the high rise apartment. The sky was blue with only a couple of white fluffy clouds up high in the sky. It was as though the sun were pushing the greyness of winter out of the way and the previously "dead" trees were now tinged with green. This safe, cocooned room felt too small on that day, almost suffocating. So I grabbed a coat and headed for the lifts to take me down to earth.

The constant sound of the jackhammers and other building equipment was much louder than in the apartment, where the 24-hour noise was muffled by double-glazed windows. It was a perpetual background noise, as Shanghai pursued its Western makeover. I crossed the road and made my way to the back streets where there are less cars and I could stroll along at the relaxed Chinese walking pace.

I passed one of the worksites. Another block of old traditional Shanghainese shikumen houses had been demolished. The typical narrow red bricks were being cleaned and stacked up neatly at the side. Three women wearing loose trousers, shirts and head scarves sat on tiny stools tapping the bricks carefully with tools to rid them of the old mortar. Next to the stack of bricks were the old wooden doors. Some still had the glass in them, but mostly they had square designs cut through the wood. Next to the doors were the piles of scrap metal that had been the reinforcing rods. Nothing was wasted on these sites. Most of this material would be sold or would find its way into new buildings.

Beyond the ladies were the workmen. I walked very slowly, trying to take in as much through the gap in the building fence as I could. It seemed rude and callous to stand around in my clean expensive clothes staring at these hard-working labourers. There were at least 60 men, all wearing orange helmets, which introduced some colour to the grey, dusty demolition site. I saw the flash of a welding arc, but the man was not wearing a protection shield over his eyes. I lingered for a moment, wondering how his eyes could take it. Later I asked my metallurgist husband about this, because I knew that to get arc burn in your eyes was extremely painful and could lead to blindness. He told me that the men just shut their eyes when the arc went on, opening them in between to see where to weld the next bit.

I noticed a few of the workmen looking at me, and I looked back at them for a moment before walking on. I was wondering what they were thinking. Deep lines were etched into their young faces; their thin muscular bodies carried their clothing loosely as if it was originally for a bigger frame. They returned to lifting big hunks of rock and broken concrete by hand into wheelbarrows and depositing them over at the edge of the building site.

How could I feel so miserable? I did not have to work, and when I did, I never worked as hard as these people. I had plenty to eat, which was evident from my rather too rounded body, and had a variety of clothes and shoes to wear. The places in which I lived were spacious, clean, and warm or cool depending on the season, with décor that created a pleasant atmosphere.

Guilt attached to my sadness. I heard the voice in my head lecturing me, "I've got nothing to feel sad about. Just look around. People toil and struggle to make a meagre living. How would I feel if I had to swap places with them? Then I really might have something to feel miserable about!"

I crossed over another road, at the pedestrian lights. Even though the little green walk sign had appeared and pedestrians had begun to walk across, a couple of cars rushed through as if the red light was just "suggesting" they stop rather than "insisting". No one complained, so I began to cross. Cars, motorbikes and carts piled up with every imaginable thing were allowed to turn through the pedestrians at any time. Most did not bother to stop for the foot traffic, so we had to stop and start and weave our way through them. Pleased that I had once again survived a Chinese road crossing, I continued past the park and turned down another street in which the bamboo scaffolding of another building site covered the road like a pergola. Each bamboo pole was attached to another bamboo pole with flat plastic twine. Bamboo is very strong, waterproof and does not rot. I had imagined that a bamboo pole was hollow. But if you look down into a pole, you cannot see further than about ten centimetres. On the outside, equally spaced down the pole, there are lines running horizontally. Initially I thought they were just superficial marks on the surface, but they actually mark where a little internal "shelf" of flat bamboo is, which forms a solid circle inside the pole. This gives the bamboo its strength – a natural reinforcement.

Materials were being passed hand to hand up and down the scaffolding. The men were standing on plaited bamboo mats that could be shifted easily to where they were needed. Seven men on the ground were heaving an air compressor onto a wooden cart drawn by a tricycle. One of the men hopped on the bike and pedalled over to another part of the site, where seven more men lifted it off again. Low labour costs militated against the use of modern mechanical marvels. I could not see any forklifts or pickup trucks or cement mixers. It was all being done by hand.

Just at the edge of the fence was a group of five men sitting on tiny stools eating lunch. Each had a small bowl, some with rice topped with fish or chicken, while others had soup with noodles and vegetables.

A Dutch friend of mine told me that when her father, who worked on road construction, went off to work in the morning, he took with him a whole loaf of bread, meat fillings for the sandwiches, fruit and cake. The comparison between the cultures was as startling as it was shocking.

The voice in my head accused me again. "You've never had to go hungry in your life. You eat until you're full at every meal. You should be more grateful and stop feeling morose."

Making up part of the fence were three shipping containers stacked on top of each other. Windows had been cut out at the side for air which enabled me to look inside. I saw rows of bunk beds with clothes draped over the end. Other clothes were drying on coat hangers at the windows or were threaded through poles that hung out over the street. (At times I'd been dripped on by clothes hanging on poles over other streets.)

The bunks were never empty. When one man climbed out to start work, another one fell into it after completing the preceding shift. On many building sites the work went on around the clock. I noticed a couple of women cooking on little burners inside one of the containers. These must have been the wives visiting from rural areas where most of these workers were from. Farm work was becoming increasingly difficult and less profitable, so millions of people were flooding into the big cities in the hope of finding jobs with better pay to help support the family. Usually a husband and wife only saw each other once or twice a year. If a couple had both moved to the city, often their child would stay behind with the grandparents and would not see their parents until National Week in October, or the New Year celebrations around February.

The men who came from the rural areas often found work at construction sites, while the women would become an *ayi* (pronounced "eye ee"). This is the word for auntie. In traditional Chinese culture, unmarried or widowed women would help serve the extended family with cooking, cleaning and childcare. Present day *ayis* do the same, only they often travel thousands of miles from their small communities to a megacity where they work for wealthy Chinese or foreigners.

More internal accusations filled my head.

"Imagine having to leave my own precious child and go thousands of miles away to look after strangers' children and only get to see my child once a year. I didn't even need to leave them to go to work. I've had it so easy. It's just wrong to feel so sad."

When these "migrant workers" leave their country districts, they are not entitled to the usual benefits from the government such as health care, housing assistance or education for the children. That is why the children have to be left behind.

After strolling past unattractive building sites, I decided to walk back through one of the many beautiful parks. With the obvious influence of feng shui, the parks are landscaped with lush foliage of many different shades of green, layering towards the paved pathways with contrasting borders like burgundy fittonias. In season the hydrangeas, camellias and azaleas produce masses of blooms. Some of the bigger parks have large man-made ponds with small running streams meandering through adjoining parks, over which are placed wooden arched bridges. Gliding regally over the lakes are white swans, geese and ducks. Each season, beds of prolific annuals smile at you – pansies, bonfire salvias and petunias in the autumn, impatience and marigolds in the summer, and a plethora of colourful bulbs in the spring. Dotted throughout the parks are perfectly placed trees like Japanese maples, cumquats, willows and even palm trees.

Just before I entered Huai Hai Park, I paused momentarily. This park used to be a cemetery and I assumed the bodies were still there underneath us. I wondered whether some of the spirits were not happy about being disturbed and were hovering around, cranky and revengeful. I said a special prayer for the departed and entered the park, walking a little way until I reached a shady part. Big plane trees formed a canopy shading bench seats and exercise equipment. Even in winter people congregated on these seats. Some were chatting and smoking, others relaxed while they watched the activities and observed the people as they walked through the park. A few people were lying down on the benches, sleeping. A little further on were numerous tables and chairs where small groups of people were playing cards while another 10 or 15 men hovered around observing the game, puffing on cigarettes. The tobacco smoke encircled the group like vaporous spirits. Around the perimeter of this area was bright blue and green exercise equipment which was always in use. People of every age were running, balancing, pulling, leaning, and bending, as they exercised every part of the body. Once I observed a very old lady, who looked every bit of 90 years old, with her leg stretched horizontally up on the bar. Another day a frail old man was doing balancing exercises.

Usually at about 6.15 in the morning Rob and I went walking in another park nearby. It would be full of people exercising, especially the elderly. They stood in groups, stretching their legs and placing them on elevated objects like benches or fences as they proceeded to punch the top and bottom of their knees with their hands. I assumed it was to keep the blood circulating. Other people did graceful *Tai Chi* in perfect unison. *Chi* is understood by the Chinese as the positive force in the universe, responsible for health, energy and strength. *Tai Chi* is a gentle martial art that harnesses the *Chi* within the body. Around the path were groups of men and women jogging together, sweating, talking and laughing. For a number of months we had to battle for a place on the paths as about 30 young firemen trainees underwent their training. Jogging or sprinting, they carried big heavy fire hoses while dressed in all their long-sleeved gear, which caused them to sweat profusely. Many of them struggled to complete the circuit, only to be told by their superior with a stopwatch and cigarette in the corner of his mouth, to do another circuit.

It was a wonderful morning activity, marred by the one thing that I do not think I will ever get used to. The Chinese, like many Asians, do not believe in using a handkerchief. They think it is disgusting to put all that stuff back into your pocket. They prefer to blow their nose contents and spit their throat mucus onto the ground, usually preceded by a good deep guttural drawback. It is a matter of keeping your eye on the path ahead to miss all the little glistening blobs dotted along the ground.

As I continued my walk through Huai Hai Park, I needed to dodge a couple of people walking backwards. This apparently exercised different muscles and helped with balance. Another woman was facing a tree and continuously bowed up and down with her hands closed together in a praying position.

I followed a man wheeling his bicycle into another area canopied by trees. Two bamboo birdcages were secured on the back of his bikes. As he removed the blue material covers, the birds began to sing. He carried the cages to one of the trees, and he then hooked them onto a branch. I noticed eight other cages hanging on nearby trees. The birds were quite big and sang loudly as the people sat around listening to them. I had also seen much smaller cages containing shrill crickets. One day in a taxi, the driver had his cricket with him. I found the noise piercing in the confines of the car, but he obviously enjoyed it.

Since I had arrived in China I had often felt afraid. The sheer number of people, the constant noise and congestion of this megacity, with strong unfamiliar smells from food and drains, could be overpowering. I had also internalised some warnings given to me by well-meaning people, some of whom had been Chinese themselves, from Hong Kong.

"You can't trust the people in mainland China," was the constant advice before we arrived.

"You have to be very, very careful with your belongings, as they will try and steal from you and rip you off. When my aunt and I visited the mainland a few years ago, we were really quite terrified at times," advised a well-intentioned friend from Hong Kong. I had also read a number of books about the tumultuous years of the Cultural Revolution, the Great Leap Forward and other equally disastrous initiatives by Chairman Mao Tse-tung, where the people were "educated" to despise the West.

Therefore, throughout my stay I had been clutching my handbag in front of me, often looking straight ahead, so that I did not have eye contact with anyone who might take advantage of me.

But during this afternoon that attitude changed. I could hear music coming from deeper in the park, so I stopped to watch a group of ordinary people singing and dancing. Three elderly men were sitting on a low brick wall. They had traditional instruments. One was like a small violin with one string over which a bow is guided, called an *erhu*. Another played a *pi pa* which is similar to a lute, and the third a *di zi*, which sounds like a flute. Up until now I had not enjoyed traditional music, but that day it lured me with its haunting melodies. I wandered over to where a small group of people were watching some women and a man dancing to the music. I was captivated by the elderly man who I imagined must have once been a professional dancer. He was tall and willowy, moving gracefully around the area with ease and confidence. His eyes were shut and he appeared to be in his own world, maybe transported to another time and place, maybe back to his youth before he was deprived of this pleasure. Between 1966 and 1976, during the Cultural Revolution, Mao Tse-tung passed a directive to do away with the "Four Olds" referred to as back elements. These were old ideas, old culture, old customs and old habits.

What I was observing would have been totally forbidden less than 30 years before.

I was roused from my musings by one of the female dancers dressed in an orange and black tartan pantsuit with auburn dye through her "up do" hair. She stood in front of me smiling, nodding and holding out her hand towards me.

Oh my goodness, she wants me to dance, I realised.

"*Buo you* ... no no!" I answered, stepping backwards.

The watching crowd had turned towards me clapping and smiling encouragingly.

What have I got to lose? Nobody knows me, I thought, as I handed my bag, containing my wallet, to the woman standing next to me, defying all the warnings.

Stepping into the middle of the circle I started to mimic the dancers as they moved around in the centre of the smiling crowd. The music stopped and I went to go, but a woman came dashing over with a colourful shirt and pulled it over my head. The music started and this time the tall elderly man glided over and we danced as a pair. When he opened his eyes wide, like in a Chinese Opera, I opened mine. As he turned and twisted his arms theatrically to a known choreography, I followed. Meanwhile the crowd had more than doubled and they were hooting and clapping. When the dance ended, they all clapped and clapped. I bowed to my partner and then to the crowd, who bowed back to me.

The woman handed back my purse.

My fear of the Chinese ended that afternoon as the warmth I felt from them and towards them melted all the icy tentacles of fear. For the rest of our stay in China that warmth only increased.

This was a beam of light that shone into my cave making it less dark and sad. After this day I gradually found my way out of the cave, as this light was followed by other rays of light that further brightened the way. The rays of light came in a variety of forms. One ray was in the form of a special friendship. Another was in finding an international writers' group that helped me to pick up my pen and begin to write again. Yet another one came in the form of an invitation to teach some Chinese people about Christianity within the Catholic Church we had been attending. This led to writing for a magazine and so it went on. It was also discovered that I had an underactive thyroid, which had exacerbated any depressed feelings I had experienced since we had moved back from America. Modern medicine is a wonderful thing, and with this helping to balance my body, together with the previously mentioned rays of light, I stopped feeling so isolated and panicky about being by myself. I found I enjoyed it, as I could devote myself to my own interests without having to worry about all the day-to-day activities of caring for a family. With two maids cleaning our apartment three times a week and a variety of good cheap restaurants close by, I settled into a very different lifestyle than the one I had been living for the past 25 years and it felt good. Conquering the fear of being alone and rediscovering myself as a useful middle-aged woman continued to develop a sense of wholeness in me.

Bamboo forest

To stay in Shanghai is to see a unique side of China. It has the feel of a modern opulent city with its stylish women, nightclubs, countless restaurants, bars and shops. It is hard to realise that it is part of a communist country.

It is when you head out of this pin-up city that you can begin to appreciate how the majority of Chinese people live. On a trip to Anhui Province we visited the rural village of a friend's *ayi* (maid) called Huan-yue. Through this we were given a unique insight into rural life.

After driving for many hours we turned down a side road that until quite recently had been a dirt track. About one and a half kilometres later, we arrived at the beginning of a bamboo forest. We parked the car and walked into the forest, down a slippery, shaded track to a little concrete home. We were welcomed by the *ayi*'s parents-in-law who had invited us for lunch. This elderly couple were bringing up Huan-yue's child, while she worked as a maid in Shanghai. We walked through a dark doorway to the middle of the three-room house which was the living/dining room. It consisted of unpainted concrete walls and floor with a few posters for decoration, including Chairman Mao, and a calendar from a few years ago. Along the back wall was a simple sideboard upon which was a plain clock and three thermos flasks filled with hot water for tea.

We were ushered to a square wooden table covered with an orange floral plastic cloth around which were four bench seats. Mother-in-law went to the small kitchen to the left to bring out dishes of vegetables, rice, fish and a thin soup. The doors near where we were sitting opened out onto a small concrete area. A large plastic bowl of water, in which they did the washing up, was on the ground. Next to that was a neat vegetable garden, and beyond, a thick bamboo forest. Wet clothes were hanging on a bamboo pole supported by two other bamboo poles.

After lunch we were taken on a walking tour of the local area by Father-in-law. He took us along the dirt track for about 20 metres, where we came to an identical house with its vegetable garden and a small wired-off area for the chickens. This is where their son lived with his family.

Up until about ten years ago there was very little rubbish in these villages as everything was used and reused, eaten or turned into fertiliser. As the people were no longer taxed for each chicken they owned and other such petty but debilitating taxes, they could afford to buy toothpaste, medicine in bottles and extra food wrapped in plastic bags. Without any experience of what to do with rubbish, everything was thrown out the doors of the houses so that as we walked through the rest of the village, we saw rubbish strewn everywhere, even in the forest.

The villagers were very excited to have "foreigners" visiting and were friendly.

Father-in-law had been in this area for 30 years after moving from his Northern Province where millions of people were starving due to another of Mao Tse-tung's initiatives called The Great Leap Forward. This was supposed to be a five-year plan, but it was called off after just three tragic years. The period between 1958 and 1960 is known as the "Three Bitter Years" in China. Through a combination of disastrous economic policies and adverse weather conditions, an estimated 20 to 40 million people died in China. Most starved to death in the countryside.

Father-in-law took up bamboo harvesting, which he continued to do until now. He wanted to take us for a walk up the steep hill to his part of the forest. Through our friend's translation he was able to explain some interesting things about bamboo. He told us that bamboo must be at least four years old before it can be harvested and he leant down to show us some new bamboo shoots. Even at this early stage he could tell if they will grow well. If the new shoots have brown leaves on top, he removes them as these ones do not grow into strong, big bamboo. These shoots are then used for food. Bamboo keeps growing and is harvested all year round, even in the freezing months of winter. Around his waist he carried a special cutting knife which he used to harvest all these tall strong bamboos by hand. Then he dragged it all the way down the mountain and onto a cart which he then had to pull one and a half kilometres to the road. Before this little track down to the main road was sealed five years ago he had to drag the load by hand all the way down to the main road as the track could not tolerate anything with wheels. Even in the depths of winter, he dragged the heavy bamboo through the deep snow. He was proud that he could drag huge amounts of long bamboo at a time. It was hard to imagine that he could do it as he was so small and thin.

Back at the house we sat outside sipping hot green tea,

admiring the view of the forest. We said how lovely it must be to look at this nice view every day. The elderly couple shook their heads and said they did not enjoy it, as it just reminded them of their hard life.

We spent the rest of the afternoon walking through the village, invited by many people to come into their home for tea. Towards evening we headed up another small mountain to watch the sun set. We sat on a bare rock where during the hot summer evenings people would go to feel a cool breeze blowing through the forest behind them ... nature's air-conditioning.

We followed the stream back down the mountain and then crossed over a little bridge to three identical houses. The middle one was where Huan-yue's mother lived. We had been invited for dinner. She welcomed us with her enormous smile and then we sat outside drinking tea while she finished preparing the meal. Then Huan-yue presented us with beautiful handmade slippers that her mother had made for each of us. They were hand-embroidered and each pair had taken her three days to make. We were all taken aback. Here was a woman who owned very little taking the time and expense to make us these slippers. Although we had given each family a bag of goodies consisting of some food and good quality tea, this was from our surplus and was not a hardship for us. I was very humbled by her generosity and by the warmth and hospitality of all the villagers.

Dentist in China

I was not really afraid to go to the dentist. The sharp pain in my tooth, which reacted violently to heat, cold or even air, indicated to me that another root was dying under a back molar. I had been through this in Australia and America and it meant a root canal filling. An inconvenience, but with modern numbing procedures it was not really painful. After doing some research to find a reputable dentist in Shanghai, I made the appointment at a dental surgery just near where we lived. It was a chain of dentist surgeries started in China by an American company. I was pleased to observe that the reception area was clean and the staff spoke reasonable English. This indicated that they were used to dealing with foreigners.

After a short wait I was taken to small narrow room, where I sat in a typical dentist chair. The room was not as pristine as the foyer. There were cracks in the walls and the pale pink paint definitely needed a new coat. The room was devoid of anything pleasant to distract the patient; there was not even a poster of nice scenery. Presently a petite Chinese woman with a modern spiky haircut entered the room, followed by three assistants, two young men and a woman. They jammed into the small room.

"Good morning. I am Hai Ing and I will be your dentist today."

I assumed that she had earned her dentist degree in America. Many Shanghainese speak English, but the people who are very proficient have usually lived overseas for a few years. After blowing cold air onto my tooth, which sent me reeling towards the ceiling, she confirmed my diagnosis and without pause or discussion began immediately with the root canal procedure. She proceeded to ram a big wrench-like implement into my mouth to ensure it stayed wide open. I wondered if my jaws were going to dislocate.

An injection to deaden the pain did nothing to relieve the effect of the shot of cold air that was routinely blown on the poor tooth. As she was preparing the next injection, I asked, "Where did you go to university. Was it in America?"

"No, I have never been out of China. I hope to go one day."

After three more injections of anaesthetic and not even a hint of pain relief, I suggested we leave it for another day. My intention was to check this dentist out more thoroughly and also, as my mouth had been cranked open for nearly an hour and a half, it was really aching. That night my jaw was so stiff, I could hardly open it to eat. My sympathising husband made soup so I could slurp it into my mouth without having to open it too much. My jaw felt like it had been stretched beyond its capacity and I was sure it would never feel normal again.

A few days later I was back for another go, after my research validated the dentist. She was apologetic about the last time and we both felt it would go better this time. However, four injections later the tooth was still reacting to cold. It was now so sore from all the prodding that my eyes were watering uncontrollably from the pain. Finally, she placed the huge syringe down on the table. Coming around to the front of the chair she leant down towards me so that she was looking straight into my eyes as she exclaimed, "I usually work in the Chinese dentistry hospital. In a situation like this we would normally hold the patient down and do the work that needs to be done."

My heart began pounding as my mind conjured up images of people in agony being pinned to the dentist chair by unrelenting men while their teeth were pulled and huge drills ground away despite the protestations of raw nerves. I began to squirm uncomfortably in my seat as I stammered, "You've got to be kidding! Isn't there someone else that you could ask?"

I wondered if I should remind her about the big slogan written on the window outside the surgery. *"We Offer Painless Dentistry."*

Without answering me, she left the room and returned with the oral surgeon. He could not speak English and, irrationally, this made me feel more apprehensive. He felt around my mouth with his index finger and with the big syringe made three or four pricks around my gums. A few minutes later the pain had gone. And so the procedure began. It would take four more visits, and three X-rays to complete the job. I warned the rest of the roots in my mouth not to die until we left China!

As with any experience in life, be it good or bad, there is always something to be learnt. In this case it showed me that I could be brave when faced with physical pain and to be patient when things didn't go the way I expected. These were lessons that helped me prepare for what was to happen eight months later.

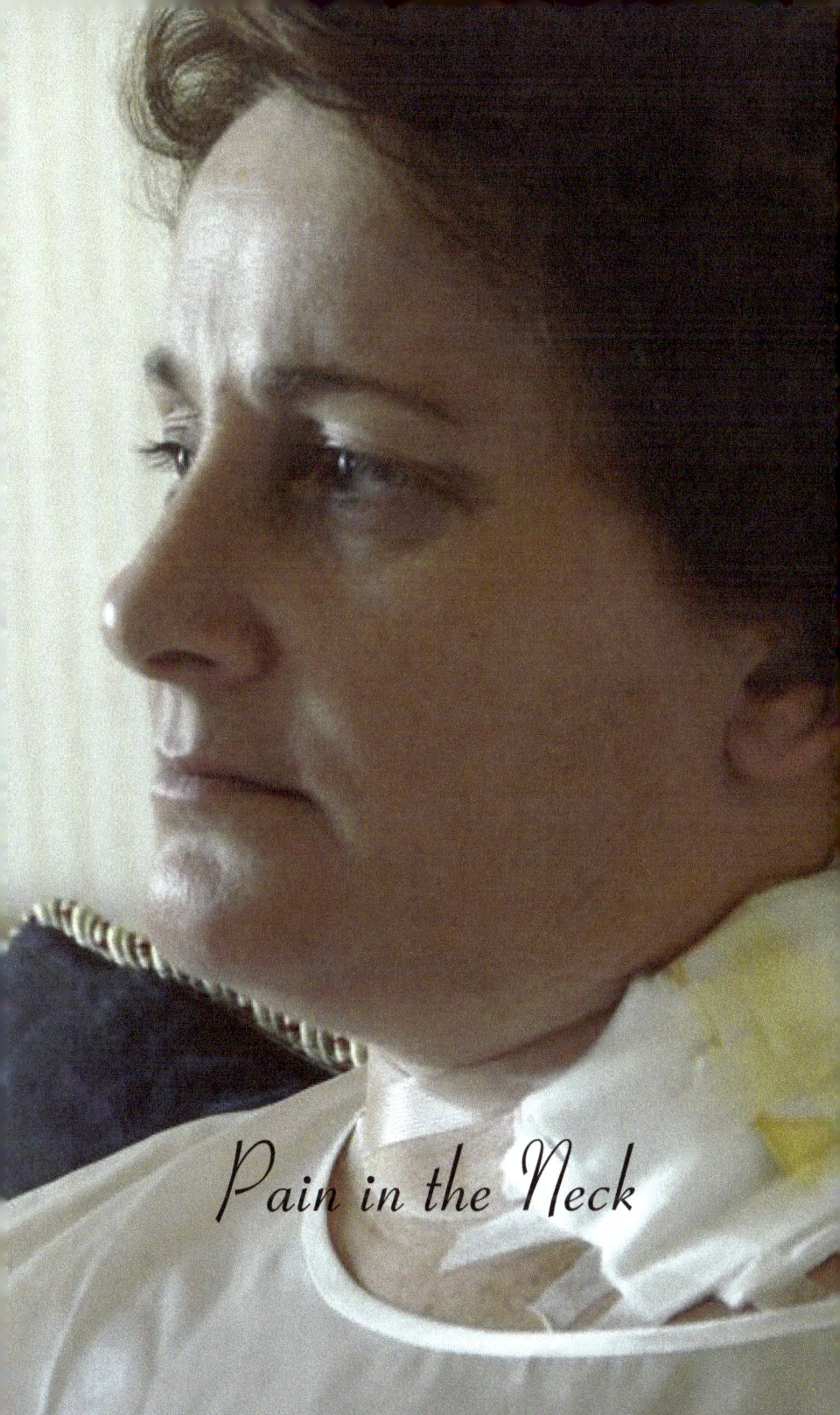

A heartbeat away

Somewhere in the distance I could hear my name being called. The voice was muffled and not quite right as it filtered through a timeless space that was not of this world, but not quite in the next. I hovered there until the voice became urgent, pleading. It pulled me towards it.

"Julie … can you hear me? … Julie … wake up!"

The voice was right next to me now as I tried to open my eyes but I did not have the strength. I had never thought about how much energy was required to open eyes.

"Heart stopped, got it going, but she's unresponsive," I heard the voice saying.

As I became more lucid, I recognised it was Dr Josey speaking, the doctor who had been attending me in the emergency department at the hospital. As she relayed the information to someone on the phone, a nurse wound the bed down so that it felt like my head was below my feet. I managed to raise my eyelids a fraction and glance around. A group of nurses with serious faces surrounded the bed. One was sticking a needle into the cannula they had put into the vein in my arm when I was admitted into the hospital less than an hour ago. Another nurse was checking the heart monitor wires stuck on my chest. I was exhausted and my eyes clamped shut as an oxygen mask was placed over my face. I listened to Dr Josey talking on the phone next to me.

"That was a close call! Her blood pressure's low and when I listen to her heart the sound is very muffled. It's obvious that the pericardium is continuing to fill with fluid and squeezing her heart. It's already stopped once."

I realised that she was talking to Dr Paul, my infectious diseases specialist who was up on the next floor of the hospital at a doctor's dinner. Feelings of guilt for interrupting him slithered through my mind, but were quickly chased out by a more relevant thought. What would have happened if I had not acknowledged that uneasy feeling that had unsettled me earlier in the evening? When my friend Sharen had rung to check on me, she insisted, against my protestations, that I should go to the hospital immediately. I had been in the emergency department for less than an hour before my heart stopped the first time.

The lump

It had been over four months since an unknown infectious disease began its march through my body. No one was sure how I got it, how it would manifest itself or how it would end. It began with a small lump on the left side of my neck. Just a weenie lump that I had felt by chance, while drinking coffee with some friends in a Melbourne café. I was returning to China in two days' time, so my local doctor decided to do an ultrasound. He was unperturbed when I called him for the results, "Just a virus in the lymph node," he said. "Should clear up soon, nothing to worry about."

On the return flight to Shanghai I stopped over in Sydney to see my son Peter who was working there. We talked for a while after dinner even though the pain in my neck was growing in intensity. During the evening Peter shared a concern that he had been trying to address for two years, but was unable to do so. As I was his mother, it became my concern too. That night in bed I could hardly move my neck for the pain, but as I thought it was just a virus that would soon improve, I continued on my return journey to China the next day.

On the plane I was seated next to an elderly Chinese lady who was obviously new to flying as she did not know how all the equipment in the seat worked. She could not speak or read English and was obviously distressed. So it became necessary for me to help by leaning over to show her how to manage the seat equipment. Unfortunately this movement greatly increased the pain in my neck. To add to my discomfort, a restless child behind me kept kicking the back of my seat, which jarred me and further aggravated my pain.

Finally the plane lights were subdued indicating that it was time for people to settle down for sleep. Soon all was quiet except for the soft droning of the aeroplane and the gentle throaty snore of someone nearby. I was unable to sleep because of my painful neck, which guided my thoughts towards the meaning of suffering. Until recently I had thought that all suffering was to be avoided and if it happened then just grin and bear it. Some people along the way had preached that you suffered if you were not praying correctly or asking for God's guidance and protection. Another more evangelical church floated an idea that it was because you had not fully submitted yourself to the Lord. Within the Hindu religion suffering was a direct result of bad karma caused by something wrong you had done in this life or in one of your past lives.

But none of these ideas had satisfied my questions about why people experienced suffering. Then I began to research Catholic theology and I heard about a radically different perspective than I had considered previously. I wanted to understand more. The first notable part that I learnt was that although nothing bad comes directly from God, at times He allows us to experience suffering for a purpose as it always leaves a person different.

"*Pain can purify and elevate the soul. It can move us to intensify our union with the divine Will. It can inspire us to* become detached from worldly goods and from excessive concern for our health. ... or it can lead us away from God leaving the soul alienated from the supernatural life."[28]

So it comes down to a choice as to how we should approach suffering when it inevitably comes to every person in one form or another in the journey of life. This was quite easy to understand, and I assumed that next time I experienced any sort of suffering I would accept it as being allowed by a God who only wanted to help me along the road of sanctity. It was easy to make that decision in my mind, but little did I know how it would soon be put to the test.

The most incredible part of this theology was harder for me to fully grasp and is best explained by Blessed John Paul II.

"In the passion and death of Christ not only is our Redemption accomplished through suffering, but also human suffering has been redeemed. From that moment on, our suffering could be united with the suffering of Christ. In this way we can participate in the Redemption of all mankind."

To fully understand this idea of redemptive suffering will probably take many more years, but I realised that suffering is not just an ordeal to get through but actually when approached with this supernatural perspective can be of enormous benefit.

As Saint Josemaria Escriva put it:

"The great Christian revolution has been to convert pain into fruitful suffering and to turn a bad thing into something good."[29]

As I sat in the silence of that aeroplane, I quietly prayed a little prayer asking if the pain in my neck could be "offered

---

28 *In conversations with God* by Francis Fernandez.
29 *Furrow* by Saint Josemaria Escriva.

up" to help my son resolve his longstanding problem. Immediately I "heard" a gentle voice speak to me. It was not audible in the normal sense but heard as clearly within my heart as if it had been.

"Would you be prepared to take on a little more suffering for that purpose?"

Without hesitation I wholeheartedly answered, "Yes!"

The operation

After what felt to me like a very long flight, the plane finally arrived in Shanghai. It was like every situation had conspired to make this journey more painful. We landed just ahead of a big thunderstorm which brought with it a tropical downpour. The bag handlers were waiting until the storm passed to unpack the plane and so we all had to wait for two hours to collect our baggage. There was nowhere to sit so I perched on the side of the bag carousel trying to support my aching neck and head. Finally, late at night, I arrived back at our apartment and collapsed into bed. The next morning I awoke with a lemon-sized lump on the side of my neck, shivering one moment, sweating profusely the next. Pain was shooting hot needles up into my head.

A week later I was in a Shanghai hospital, having the abscess lanced and drained.

That day, my son resolved his two-year problem.

I was in the part of the hospital reserved for Westerners. My private room and bathroom were brightly painted and spacious. From the spotless window, which provided plenty of natural light, I could look out onto a small garden and with the push of a button eager nurses rushed in to attend any of my needs. From this perspective I thought that the Chinese hospital was very good. Then, prior to the operation, the surgeon requested a scan of my neck, so seated in a wheelchair I was taken about 25 metres along a corridor into the Chinese part of the hospital. The walls in this part of the hospital appeared dirty, but probably just needed paint. The furniture was old with some broken chairs shoved into the corner under a smeared window, while the waiting room was crowded with miserable, sick people. Those unable to find a seat leant against the wall or crouched on the ground in family groups. Out of the corner of my eye, I saw their heads turn in unison to watch me as I was wheeled past, a bit of a distraction for a few seconds. Feelings of guilt surfaced, just like they did each time a beggar held out a dinted cup or a knarred hand, hoping that the rich Western woman will drop a few "kwai" in his direction.

The nurse parked my wheelchair outside a room and left. As I waited in that grey, impersonal corridor with my lemon-sized lump, I felt so alone. Homesickness engulfed me as thoughts turned to my mother, as they usually did when I was sick. I wanted to cry. I wanted to shut my eyes and wake up back home in Australia with Mother wiping my feverish brow with a warm flannel scented with 4711 perfume.

"The alcohol in the perfume helps to bring the temperature down," she used to say.

Before I could indulge in some relieving tears, someone jerked the brake off the wheelchair and I was propelled into the scan room. Six people were in the room attending to various things. Two of them were cleaning up a table right next to the scanner. Bloody sheets and bandages stained with other excretions of yellow and brown were being bundled up. If I was not feeling so ill, I would have attempted to flee, but just then a large man in a white coat, with the undone buttons revealing jeans and a T-shirt, began talking gruffly to me in Chinese as he pointed to the hard plastic bed that slid under the scanner. I tried to get off the wheelchair but the pain in my head and neck made moving difficult. Two other young men grabbed me under the arms and almost threw me onto the bed. I tried to lie down flat but it was too painful, so one of the young men hastened the process with a rough shove against my shoulder. Pain shot its hot needles through my head and the rest of my neck ached and tensed as I lay in this position. Looking up at the ceiling I noticed the plaster was peeling off in great chunks and water stains covered the rest. The big man was attempting to put the contrast dye into my cannula, but it was stinging and not going in. Roughly, he ripped it out, and then like a person playing darts he threw another needle into my vein.

"Be gentle!" I screamed in agony and anger, knowing he could not understand me. Even though the pitch at which I yelled to him would have informed him of the meaning, he did not even look up but continued with what he was doing. As he pulled the needle out, he flung my arm back towards me.

I felt the dye heating my body as the bed moved under the scanner. The rotating scanner buzzed over my head. It stopped for a moment and then started again. The heat from the dye had reached between my legs and I felt like I had wet my pants. I felt embarrassed and wondered what I should do, but the sensation passed and I realised that I had not. After the scan was over I needed help to sit up, and as I lunged towards the wheelchair, another woman with terror in her eyes lay down immediately on the scanning bed.

The morning following the surgery, Dr Lei, my surgeon,

came in to do what I thought was a post-operative check. He was tall for a Chinese man, yet slender, with a quiet dignity. Grey hairs outnumbered the black and numerous fine lines deepened around his eyes when he concentrated. His voice was soft as he addressed the three little nurses hovering next to him holding a tray of instruments, a large bottle of brown liquid and fresh bandages. They smiled sympathetically as they angled my head to one side and placed a plastic sheet under my chin. Dr Lei tilted the light to shine directly on my neck and leant down close. He undid the dressings and then began probing the fresh wound with a hard cold instrument. There had been no explanation or warning and the pain was sudden and intense. I instinctively grabbed his arm.

"Yow, ow, it's hurting, please stop!" I said, sobbing and trying to move to the other side of the bed away from him.

Dr Lei straightened up and talked briefly in Chinese to the nurses who were immobilised by my unexpected outburst. Then he looked at me with kind eyes and with a gentle empathetic voice explained in his limited English, "Sorry it hurt, but need to clean. It very bad abscess, near vital nerves and blood vessel. Must keep clean, so no more infection. Wound open. Not stitch it closed. This standard procedure with abscess. Keep open, stop more infection. Must keep clean. Sorry."

I let go of his arm and like a disobedient child who has been reprimanded and then submits to authority, I allowed Dr Lei to proceed.

He began to clean the open wound by pouring the brown liquid into it and then stuffing it with treated gauze before bandaging it up again. It required precision as he skilfully manoeuvred the instruments to remove the gauze from the previous day and carefully reinserted the fresh lot. It was a slow procedure that forced tears out of my eyes and made me tremble.

He kept whispering gently to me, "Not long, nearly finished, nearly finished."

Each morning, for the next three weeks Dr Lei and I would meet for this agonising procedure. After I was released from the hospital we continued to meet at the day surgery. Unfortunately my husband could not come with me during the week and so I would wait alone in the little room for Dr Lei to arrive. He would greet me with a sympathetic smile as he went to prepare his instrument tray. In keeping with his position as the leading surgeon at the hospital, he bore an air of dignity and quiet self-assurance. But on his feet he wore large bright blue plastic "crocs". His steady talented hands and elegant demeanour argued with his comical feet.

When he began the cleansing procedure, however, there was little to laugh about. Except for the offer from the assisting nurse of a small delicate hand to grasp, there was nothing to deaden the pain. The first time I squeezed her poor little hand, it was so intense that I was afraid it might break her fingers. I had wondered why they did not offer me any analgesic until I learnt that the Chinese believe that people should *bear their own pain.*

Delia was one of my closest friends in China. We met in a supermarket while I searched for gravy and we fast became friends. She had been holidaying back home in America for the summer and was not due back in China for another six weeks. The week after I got out of hospital the phone rang.

"Delia, you're back. But you weren't supposed to be back for another month."

"I know, I should still be at home on vacation with my daughter and grandkids at the beach, but one of the pipes burst in our apartment here, so I've come back to help my husband clear it up."

"I'm so glad you're back," I managed to say as tears forced their way to the surface. Feeling so alone and frightened and physically weakened by the operation and the wound cleaning each day had left their mark on my fragile emotions. But the tears were more than that. They came as I realised that this was one of those moments in which I was being looked after. As it turned out, her apartment was not badly damaged so she had not really been needed for this. But both Delia and I realised that she had been brought back to China because I really needed her.

Each day she would accompany me to see Dr Lei, and hold my hand as she whispered encouragements and prayers while I endured the wound cleaning. She made sure I had food in the house and generally supported me.

Nobody in China could decide what caused the lump. More small lumps began to develop above the open wound and on the other side of my neck, so it was decided that I should head home to Australia for investigation.

The disease takes hold

Once I was back in Australia, many strange things started occurring within my body and nobody quite knew what would happen next. Over the ensuing weeks, this elusive infection caused the lining around my heart, the pericardium, to increase with excess fluid. I found it increasingly difficult to breathe; walking had decreased to a laboured hobble to the bathroom. Throughout it all I felt surprisingly peaceful, except for one evening when I began to feel unsettled and anxious. My husband Robert had returned to China and the only person at home was my 20-year-old son Steve. He had gone out for the evening as he often did, and normally this signalled the time for me to settle down by reading a book or watching a movie. But this night fear unexpectedly began to squeeze its icy fingers around my emotions, the squeeze growing tighter and tighter as the night wore on. I lay propped up in bed trying to distract myself by watching television, but this feeling kept growing.

The phone rang. It was my friend Sharen.

"How are you?" she asked.

I explained how unsettled I felt.

"I think you need to go back to hospital tonight," said Sharen.

"Oh no. I don't really want to. I thought I'd sleep here tonight and go tomorrow."

I had been in hospital off and on over the last few months and was not in a hurry to go back. Sharen, usually not at all pushy, became quite insistent.

"No, I want you to go and pack your little bag and go to hospital. You ring Dr Paul and I'll ring the doctors at emergency and tell them you are on your way. Can you get a ride or shall I pick you up?"

She left no room for argument, so I dutifully called Dr Paul who agreed with the decision to head for hospital. He was monitoring me closely, unsure about the direction this unknown infection was going to take, and had given me his mobile phone number so I could call at any time. This gave me a great sense of security and showed me that he was not going to let this infection win. I packed my bag and called Steve to drive me to the hospital.

An hour later I was in cubicle nine of the emergency department, wired up with heart monitors and a cannula threaded up to a vein in my arm. Steve had left about 15 minutes earlier when suddenly an unusual heat burned over my body as if someone was pouring hot water on me. I started to vomit and it seemed like people were moving in slow motion around the ward. They became more and more distant until everyone disappeared. I awoke to see a nurse hovering over me and Dr Josey was jabbing a drug into the cannula. I was not sure what had happened, but the nausea had gone and the people were moving normally again. Not long after, I felt the same weird heat through my body. This time it appeared that everyone grew smaller and took on a grey misty appearance. I had the buzzer in my hand and held it down as the blackness engulfed me. My heart had stopped a second time in less than half an hour. I could hear voices and felt myself being moved around but I was too exhausted to care.

After a while I felt myself being wheeled along a corridor and then we stopped. I opened my eyes briefly and saw the "Radiology" sign. The poor radiologist had been called back to the hospital at this hour to do an ultrasound on my heart. At one point during the scan, the radiologist pushed a button and I heard the sound of my heart beating. It was quite muffled but it was beating steadily. It occurred to me that this muscle was beating away every second of every day without a thought from me. What if that next beat did not come? My life would be over. At that moment I recognised that every beating heart is a mini miracle. Most other muscles get tired and need a rest. Even lungs can stop for a short time if we hold our breath. But a heart just keeps beating tirelessly in the background.

Soon after the scan I was taken to intensive care and put in the isolation ward. Everyone who came in had to put protective clothing on, including a mask, because my disease was undiagnosed. "Suspected" tuberculosis and other infectious diseases were listed on the chart.

The staff were following standard procedure, but I felt so alone and contaminated as eyes looked at me through filtering masks and hands touched me with rubber gloves. As they walked out of my room, all outer garments were removed and placed into a sealed container. I was hesitant to press the call button as it required the nurse to spend a good five minutes donning all the gear.

"It appears that the pericardium is filling up with fluid rapidly now. It's squeezing your heart, reducing its ability to pump," said a doctor I had not seen until then.

He was young but had an air of confidence and authority. Although he looked at me kindly, I could tell, by the way he kept checking and rechecking my charts and monitors and reminding me to tell him if I felt any different, that he was worried. "We need to operate and drain the fluid out of the pericardium and cut a small 'window' in it to allow any further fluid to drain out," he explained.

"It sounds serious, is it dangerous?" I was getting the sense that I was sicker than I had thought.

"Well, put it this way, it will be more dangerous if we don't. Now the problem is, do we call the surgeon and anaesthetist in now or wait until morning? If we can, it's probably better to wait until morning. You are being closely monitored so if there are any more problems we will have to call them in immediately. You must tell me if you feel any different."

"Does my husband know what's happening? He's in China. Can I call him?"

"Yes, I think we need to do that. Is there anyone else we should call?"

"But it's the middle of the night, I feel bad. Maybe my sister. No, maybe I'll call her in the morning."

He went to say something, but changed his mind and checked the heart monitor.

"We'll organise a phone so that you can call your husband."

I could see three men talking outside my room, one of whom was Dr Paul. They kept looking in my direction and finally Dr Paul came in.

I was really pleased to see him and felt safer now that he was here. It was a few months now since I had met him at my first appointment and as he examined me I visualised him as a doctor in Africa or another Third World country. He had a sparse short beard and greying hair that was longer than a traditional doctor's short back and sides. His eyes were bright blue and they focused on me intently as I answered his questions. He ordered countless tests and explained each result to me thoroughly so that together we could try and track the course of this nebulous disease.

"You've had quite an exciting night of it, haven't you?" he said as he came and stood near the bed in my isolation unit.

"Yes. It's all a bit hazy though."

"You made the right decision to come into hospital, that's for sure. I've told the nurses on this ward that they can do away with all the isolation rigmarole. You're not infectious."

"That's good. I do feel a little like a leper."

He flashed a cheerful smile at me in reply.

"So have they explained what's going on?" he asked.

"Yes. I think they've decided to wait until morning before they operate, is that right?"

"At this stage, yes, but we'll keep monitoring you. They're keeping me up to date."

As he turned to leave, a familiar face appeared. It was Kenny, Sharen's husband, who had been working on the emergency ward where I had been admitted earlier. It was now two o'clock in the morning and I knew his shift had ended two hours ago.

"Kenny, you're still here?"

"Yes, I didn't want to leave until I knew how you were doing."

Dr Paul gave Kenny a quick synopsis of my condition and left.

"Thank you so much, Kenny. What a night! They want to operate on my heart. It sounds scary."

"It has been an eventful night, but you are in very good hands. There are some excellent people keeping an eye on you."

After a while Kenny left for home and within the hour Sharen appeared.

"Oh Sharen, it's such a relief to see you, but it's three o'clock in the morning. You'll be so tired."

"No, it's fine. Kenny woke me and told me what was happening and we both felt I should be here. I was scrambling around in the dark but wanted to bring you something. I found this. It's been blessed."

With that she handed me a little crucifix that I clasped tightly for the rest of the night as I continued to offer up this time of suffering for any divine purpose. I was feeling too distracted to be more specific.

Early the next morning as I was being wheeled to surgery one of the nurses explained the procedure.

"I just want to prepare you," she puffed as she attempted to keep up with the fast-paced orderly who was wheeling my trolley. "With very sick patients, as you are, it's sometimes difficult to give a full anaesthetic, so we may just have to give you a local."

"You mean I will be awake for this?"

"It's a strong possibility."

I gripped the crucifix firmly as tears formed a watery glaze through which I viewed the preparation room. I lay passively as more blood tests were taken and injections given. Once in the operating room, I saw the surgeon who had visited me earlier, now in his surgical greens waiting to begin the operation.

I leant up on the elbow that was not burdened with cannulas and tubes and said with a touch of panic, "I thought you said you wouldn't hurt me!"

"I won't."

"But the nurse said I would have to be awake for this procedure."

"Good heavens, I wouldn't do this operation without a full anaesthetic."

"Oh thank God. But why would the nurse …"

The anaesthetist put a needle in the tube, and as I went under, the irritation I felt at spending the last half hour worrying unnecessarily was cut short.

I awoke to find a thick hose coming out of my chest, which ran down into a container beneath the bed. For the next four days it was difficult to distinguish between sleep and consciousness. They both happened in such rapid succession that the days seemed surreal. Everything was an effort and everything exhausted me. When family came to visit, in less than five minutes I drifted off to sleep. When phone calls came, I could only listen to a few sentences and the phone would begin to slip out of my hand. I was too weak to hold it to my ear, even though I was lying down and the phone was resting on the pillow. Talking was exhausting, which was understandable, but I realised that sometimes it takes even more energy to listen.

The days came and went and finally I was allowed out of intensive care back onto the ward. During the following week I underwent more scans and tests, including a bone marrow biopsy, as the medical teams tried to identify this disease. As most of the tests needed weeks to grow the cultures, I had to take numerous medications both orally and intravenously to attack a variety of possible diseases. We could not wait for a specific diagnosis to begin treatment; it would have been too late.

When I went home, I found it difficult to swallow all the tablets and a number of times I just could not keep them down. Nauseous and weak, I lay in bed day after day wondering if I would ever feel normal again. Family and friends dropped in bringing food and help. My 87-year-old mother, herself struggling with worn-out knee joints, irregular heart and limited lung capacity, carried a bowl of her chicken soup on a tray. Next she brought in a bowl of warm water and a flannel.

"I can't do much, but I have to do something to help. A sponge-down can be soothing even though I haven't got any 4711 perfume to put in it," she said as she sat down on the bed next to me and proceeded to gently wipe my face, arms and legs and rub in some fragrant lotion.

This loving gesture of human touch imbued warmth and comfort into my disease-ravaged body which for weeks had only known pain from needles and operations. As I lay there feeling so unwell, I had no idea that in a few days I was going to experience what I believe was a miracle.

Rapid recovery

Every month for the past couple of years, ten of my closest friends and I would get together. We'd have lunch, and share our joys and struggles, relishing the special bond and understanding that true friendship brings. We had named the group Amichea, which is Latin for "a meeting of women". It was time for our December get-together and one of the women offered to drive me.

"Why not give it a go, it might be good to get out for a while," said Stephanie.

"I'd really like to, but I don't know how I'd go, I still feel so sick and pretty weak."

Stephanie was not about to give up.

"Even if you only go for half an hour, I'm very happy to bring you home as soon as you want."

"Well, OK. That sounds good. Thanks, Steph."

A couple of days later, we arrived at the get-together. I managed to sit up talking for about 20 minutes and then I just had to lie down. After a while I came out and chatted for another short time until the waves of fatigue and nausea forced me to lie down again. This went on for a couple of hours until I asked to go home. Just before we dispersed, a suggestion was made that they say a prayer for me. I flopped into a chair grateful for their kindness but convinced that nothing was ever going to help me feel better. My friends gathered around and lovingly placed their hands on me. The short prayer was for healing and although I do not doubt that people experience these unexplained cures, I knew that it would not work for me. After our goodbyes, I staggered out to the car to be driven home. I just managed to make it inside and collapsed into bed.

    The next morning I woke to a clear sunny day. Instead of lying there feeling exhausted, I got up and realised that I was feeling hungry for the first time in weeks. As I walked to the kitchen I decided that the house could do with some cleaning. I had previously felt too ill to bother or even to notice it. After a good breakfast I began to clean the house. It was as I was vacuuming the hallway that it dawned on me. I no longer felt nauseous and I had energy. I switched off the vacuum cleaner and gazed through the window onto the garden. I watched a couple of wattle birds pushing their long beaks into a flower to get to the nectar. How could I have felt so ill only 18 hours earlier, with barely enough strength to have a shower, let alone clean this big house? And that awful nausea had gone.

    The wattle birds flew off as I walked towards the window and I leant on the bench beneath it watching a few white clouds float across the sky. Then it came to me. The prayer, the short prayer said by my friends yesterday, had resulted in such a quick transformation. I had experienced a miracle. I made a cup of tea and sat down to ponder on the last six months. It had been a tumultuous time of sickness and pain. But this was not what was going through my mind. Instead I was remembering all the kindness and care I had experienced from people here and overseas. The medical staff had all been so kind and thorough and friends had gone out of their way to help in a variety of thoughtful ways. I had been kept buoyed by them and felt an underlying sense of peace throughout the whole ordeal. This, I concluded, was what was meant by God's love in the world. He does not just drop things out of the sky but works through people, be it doctors, nurses or friends. He used a group of women to bring what I now understood was His healing touch. The other miracle, I learnt a few weeks later, was that there was no permanent scarring around my heart or lungs, which was completely unexpected.

So with this news I felt ready to return to China where Rob and I remained for another two and a half years. This was followed by a year in Singapore until we decided to return home.

Finding My Vocation

"The discovery of one's personal vocation is the most important point in each person's existence. It changes everything without changing anything; just as a landscape, without changing, is different before and after the sun goes down, beneath the light of the moon, or wrapped in the darkness of night. Every discovery gives a new beauty to things, and a new light creates new shadows; one discovery is the prelude to other discoveries of new lights and more beauty."[30]

Mary of Nazareth by Federico Suarez.

The half person no longer

Returning home after five years meant another readjustment, but this time it all went smoothly. Spending time with our family and friends we settled into the next phase of life. I recognised my new role as one of the "sandwich" generation who juggle their time and energies between the two extremes of life. Our three young grandchildren, energetic and adventurous, contrasted with the ageing process of both our mothers now in their 90s.

Anne was in a similar situation, although her children were a good deal younger than mine. She had also been on a spiritual journey which had taken her in different directions to me. Although she and her family had been very involved in the Church of Christ for many years, they no longer attended. Anne had completed courses in spiritual direction and life coaching and had begun helping "pilgrims" in these areas. Then she discovered the ancient form of personality analysis known as the Enneagram. She was really drawn to this as a way to help people understand themselves and how they relate to others. After doing a number of years of training, including a couple of seminars overseas, she was now attempting to get a business going doing this work with people.

I enjoyed being home and all that it entailed, but I had a persistent thought that I should be doing something specifically for God after all the trouble He had gone to in directing me. During the years of searching for my spiritual home, the topic of finding God's will for your life was a common theme. The inference in the various churches and groups we had explored over the years was that it was the missionaries and ministers who had truly found God's purpose for their lives. Yet I longed to find this calling too as I firmly believed that each person was on this earth for a reason.

Many years earlier when I was at home raising our children, I remember a conversation I had with Rob. We had returned from the Uniting Church one Sunday where a couple of missionaries were talking about the Bible studies they were doing in Indonesia and were asking our congregation to support them and their four children to live there so they could do this work.

"Rob, what do you think about supporting those missionaries? I wanted to talk to them, but so many people crowded around them that I didn't get a chance. It must be great to do God's will."

In the back of my mind I had concluded that I was marking time until my children were older and then I could pursue something more significant for God.

Rob was irritated by my comment which had triggered some thoughts he had obviously been pondering on.

"That's all very well to leave your job and drag your young kids off to a far-flung place and then expect others to support you. Doing Bible studies is all well and good but what about those of us who work hard to support our families? We design and build houses for people to live in, bridges to drive over and roads to travel along. My father spent his life growing food for people. What would the world do without us? Aren't we doing God's will?"

I didn't know how to answer him at that time but what he said made an impact and stayed in my mind for the next 25 years.

Books can be a significant way of discovering new truths, especially when they have a habit of turning up at just the right time in your journey. I had been pondering the idea of saints, those totally committed inspiring people, who showed daring heroism in their lives; people beyond the average person's capabilities, or so I thought. One day I picked up a book with a provocative title, *You can become a saint*.[31] As I read, the author kept referring to a Spanish priest, Father Josemaria Escriva, who assured people that anyone can become a saint. "… this ordinary, everyday, unassuming life can be a way to holiness: you do not have to leave your place in the world to seek God, unless the Lord has given you a religious vocation; all the ways of the earth can be opportunities for an encounter with Christ." [32]

This man showed me that the way for everyone to know God's will for their lives is by understanding the marvellous reality that any honest and worthwhile work can be converted into a divine occupation. In God's service there are no second-class jobs –all of them are important.

So when I was at home with my little children working hard at being the best mother I could be, I was actually right in the heart of God's will for my life at that time. When I

---

31   By Mary Ann Budnik.
32   Saint Josemaria Escriva, March 1930.

was awakened for the third time in the night by a baby who needed yet another feed or a nappy change and instead of handling the baby roughly and being cross with it, I instead attended to his needs with tenderness, this act was pleasing to God. When my toddler accidentally spilt sticky juice on my freshly mopped floor and I patiently cleaned it up instead of yelling at the child, God was smiling at me for doing my work with love and caring for the children He had given me. So all those years I thought I was marking time to do something significant, I was actually serving Him in the best possible way.

Rob, who for year after year has faithfully set off to work to support his family, performing his tasks with honesty, treating his workers and co-workers with respect and fairness, is in the centre of God's will for his life. Actually Rob had been correct all those years ago when he recognised the value of normal everyday work, which was just as important as a missionary's or minister's work.

This was the bit of the spiritual puzzle I was looking for. Father Josemaria Escriva had founded a personal prelature[33] that I wanted to know more about. It made so much sense. Yet the name of the prelature worried me. I had read a book in which Opus Dei was conveyed as a secret society full of mischief and deceit. This was not at all what I was discovering about its mission in the world. I decided to go ahead and meet the people involved. What I found were the warmest, sincere people who wanted to bring joy and peace to the world by spreading the Christian message that every

---

33 Opus Dei is part of the Catholic Church. The name is Latin for "Work of God". Opus Dei's mission is to spread the Christian message that every person is called to holiness and that every honest work can be sanctified.

person is called to holiness and that every honest work can be sanctified.

"*Christian cheerfulness is not something physiological. Its foundation is supernatural and goes deeper than illness or difficulties. Cheerfulness does not mean the jingling of bells or the gaiety of the dance hall. True cheerfulness is something deeper, something within; something that keeps us peaceful and happy, though at times our face may be stern.*"[34]

I realised that the book I had read denigrating this work was absolute fiction. Maybe the author used "Opus Dei" for the label of his secretive cult in the book because the name sounded unusual. But it is just the Latin words for "Work of God".

Finally I feel like all the pieces of my spiritual search have been found. Not to say I will ever get to the end of discovery and learning, but at least I have found my framework. I marvel at the enormous journey that little girl who felt like half a person has taken. With every difficulty, she struggled to make that half expand and stretch and grow. I can now assure that little girl within me that it was worth it because now we have become whole.

And most importantly I have found peace.

---

34 [34] *The forge* by Saint Josemaria Escriva.

www.ingramcontent.com/pod-product-compliance
Lightning Source LLC
Chambersburg PA
CBHW040309170426
43195CB00020B/2902